DANIEL G. AMEN, MD

#1 *NEW YORK TIMES* BESTSELLING AUTHOR

CONQUER MEMORY LOSS

SECRETS TO IMPROVING YOUR BRAIN, MEMORY & LIFE

TYNDALE REFRESH™

Think Well. Live Well. Be Well.

Visit Tyndale online at tyndale.com.

Tyndale and Tyndale's quill logo, *Tyndale Refresh*, and the Tyndale Refresh logo are registered trademarks of Tyndale House Ministries. Tyndale Refresh is a nonfiction imprint of Tyndale House Publishers, Carol Stream, Illinois.

Conquer Memory Loss

Adapted from *Memory Rescue*, published in 2017 by Tyndale Momentum under ISBN 978-1-4964-2560-7.

Designed by Libby Dykstra

Published in association with the literary agency of WordServe Literary Group, www.wordserveliterary.com.

For information about special discounts for bulk purchases, please contact Tyndale House Publishers at csresponse@tyndale.com, or call 1-855-277-9400.

Library of Congress Cataloging-in-Publication Data

A catalog record for this book is available from the Library of Congress.

ISBN 979-8-4005-0613-0

Printed in the United States of America

31 30 29 28 27 26 25
7 6 5 4 3 2 1

MEDICAL DISCLAIMER

The information presented in this book is the result of years of practice experience and clinical research by the author. The information in this book, by necessity, is of a general nature and not a substitute for an evaluation or treatment by a competent medical specialist. If you believe you are in need of medical intervention, please see a medical practitioner as soon as possible.

Contents

INTRODUCTION

THE TIME IS NOW

MEMORY IS THE FABRIC OF OUR SOULS. It enables us to integrate and make sense of the experiences of our bodies, minds, and spirits. It makes us who we are and allows us to keep our loved ones close, even when they are far away. Memory houses our joys, our hurts, and all of life's lessons. It reminds us who is trustworthy and who isn't, who has helped us and whom we need to help. Memory enables us to recall the important events in our lives and keeps us centered and growing. And because it contributes to our values and outlook, it also provides us with a sense of purpose that gives our lives meaning.

Our memories are such a part of us that we often take them for granted. Yet when our memory is damaged, the costs can be high. A diminished memory can rob us of our ability to make good decisions (because we forget important life lessons) and disconnect us from those we love. Memory problems limit our success at work, steal our independence, and ultimately make us vulnerable to anyone who might take advantage of us.

When someone's mental abilities, including memory, deteriorate enough to affect daily life, we say that person has dementia. Worldwide, a new person is diagnosed with dementia every seven seconds.[1] Of the approximately 318 million Americans living today, 45 million—about 15 percent—will get Alzheimer's disease at some point in their lives. Tens of millions more will experience other forms of dementia, and 75 percent of older adults will suffer from memory problems.[2] Plus, more than 200 medication trials have failed to reverse Alzheimer's disease and other forms of dementia.[3] Given the complexity of the illness and how early it begins altering the brain, we are likely never going to have a medicine that cures it.

Yet new research suggests that it is possible to dramatically improve memory and to prevent and sometimes even reverse some forms of dementia.[4] Given how most doctors approach this issue, however, you cannot count on traditional medicine to rescue your memory.

The Old Approach to Memory Complaints

Here is a common scenario: You are having difficulty remembering conversations, forgetting where you put your reading glasses, or briefly getting lost driving in familiar areas. So you see your primary care physician or local neurologist, who asks you a few questions, gives you some short tests, orders an MRI, and tells you, "Everyone has memory problems as they age. You're normal." It's also common for family members and friends to downplay forgetfulness.

A week or so later, you meet again with your doctor, who says that the report on your MRI came back as "mild, age-appropriate brain atrophy." He or she tells you that you have mild cognitive impairment. You're reassured that it's common and that you'll likely retain your personality and long-term memory until later in the illness. You're encouraged to get your affairs in order, given a prescription for Aricept (a common memory medication that has short-term benefits but loses its effects after 18 months[5]), and told to schedule a follow-up appointment in six months. Typically, there is no discussion about eliminating risk factors through exercise, diet, supplementation, or memory-training exercises.

That's literally the extent of the workup in 80 to 90 percent of the memory-related cases that come to us at Amen Clinics from the traditional medical system. It's completely ineffective, heartbreaking . . . and unconscionable, given what we know now.

Until recently, health-care professionals assessing the presence of memory problems in patients classified their cognitive functioning as (1) normal with no symptoms; (2) mild impairment observed by patients or their families; or (3) Alzheimer's disease, in which dementia was becoming significant and getting worse.

The National Institute on Aging announced

a significant change in 2011. Based on new brain imaging data, they added a new "preclinical" level. As a result, the current staging guidelines are

1. normal;
2. preclinical: no obvious symptoms, but negative changes can be seen on biomarkers such as brain scans;
3. mild cognitive impairment; and
4. Alzheimer's disease.

Can you see the problem with the original guidelines? Long before symptoms develop, your brain may already be deteriorating, years or even decades before you realize it![6] A UCLA study found that 95 percent of people with Alzheimer's are not diagnosed until they are in the moderate to severe stages of the disorder. Yet the brain of a person diagnosed with Alzheimer's disease at age 59 likely started to show signs of deterioration by the time that person turned 30.

No matter your age, memory symptoms should be taken seriously. Developing brain fog or feeling as if your memory is slipping when you are in your forties, fifties, sixties, seventies, or even eighties is common, but it's not normal. It is a sign of impending doom.

But while it is true that memory issues are common with age, they are not inevitable. In the presymptomatic stage, when memory problems are minor, help is likely to be most effective. If you're struggling with your memory, even if it seems inconsequential, *now* is the time to get serious about your brain's health.

A Breakthrough Concept

Our decades-long experience at Amen Clinics of looking at the brain, together with the latest scientific research, has convinced me that the traditional approach to memory problems is misguided and leads to unnecessary disease and disability.

Just as many tributaries feed a river that is about to flood and destroy a community, we've discovered that there are many different causes of memory loss. It is no longer accurate to talk about mild cognitive impairment or Alzheimer's disease as single entities with single causes, just as at Amen Clinics we no longer talk about a single type of depression, addiction, ADHD, or obesity. The ability to identify and address each of the potential causes of memory problems has enabled us to develop a plan to prevent or even reverse these devastating issues.

Conquer Memory Loss will help you identify the specific factors affecting your brain health. It will then provide you with a step-by-step approach to get your memory back, strengthen it, and keep it healthy for a lifetime.

You will learn

- strategies to decrease or eliminate avoidable risks through exercises, nutritional supplementation, and diet,
- how to follow the Memory Rescue Diet (one of the most powerful weapons for memory sustainability),
- memory training and workouts to keep your brain sharp, and
- innovative strategies to enhance brain function.

Here's the good news: *Your brain's history is not its destiny.* Even if you have brain fog or trouble remembering now, it doesn't mean you always will. You can start having a better memory today. What's more, the plan I lay out to conquer memory loss will also help your energy, mood, anxiety, sleep, weight, and overall success in life. The plan will also help you decrease your risk of developing Alzheimer's disease and other forms of dementia.

The plan for conquering memory loss that I lay out in this short book is based on an insanely simple idea: The best way to sharpen your memory, reverse brain aging, and prevent Alzheimer's is to *eliminate*, *prevent*, or *treat* the risk factors that steal your mind. Almost all these risk factors are either preventable or treatable. Even those that aren't can be ameliorated with the right strategies.

You need this book if

- Your memory has never been good and now it's getting worse.
- Your memory is not as sharp as it was 10 years ago.
- You're having trouble remembering

to take medications or supplements consistently.
- You frequently misplace your keys or phone.
- You often wonder why you came into a room.
- You're embarrassed by forgetting appointments.
- You read a book or an article but don't remember much of it.
- You struggle with brain fog.
- You notice that a loved one's failing memory is interfering with everyday tasks.
- You are concerned about a family member who has been diagnosed with dementia.
- You wonder what you can do to avoid Alzheimer's, which has been diagnosed in one or more of your close relatives.

Rest assured, you don't have to do everything at once! Most people are successful when they make one simple change at a time. Once they see how easy it is and how much better they feel, they often make scores of other healthy changes.

But regardless of how long it takes to implement the program in this book, the time to conquer memory loss is not once you've been diagnosed with "mild cognitive impairment" or Alzheimer's disease. It's now. Let me show you how.

CHAPTER 1

RECOGNIZE YOUR RISK FACTORS

THE REALITY IS THIS: If you want a stellar memory, you need to know all the potential contributors that can destroy it and address each one. As Jesus told his followers, "You will know the truth, and the truth will set you free" (John 8:32). But first, at least when it comes to adopting a healthier lifestyle, the truth is likely to make you miserable! We don't like to face the truth about ourselves—our weaknesses, bad habits, and vulnerabilities. However, until we own up to them and get serious about change, our attempts will likely be fleeting, and we'll be distracted by the next popular fad.

But change we must. I truly believe that a single pill will never fix memory decline, aging, or Alzheimer's disease, because there are too many ways trouble can occur. This is a war that must be fought on multiple fronts.

I have organized the key risk factors for memory loss according to a simple mnemonic (memory device), BRIGHT MINDS:

- Blood flow
- Retirement/aging
- Inflammation
- Genetics
- Head trauma
- Toxins

- Mental health issues
- Immunity/infection issues
- Neurohormone deficiencies
- Diabesity
- Sleep issues

You can review your own risk factors by taking the BRIGHT MINDS inventory in appendix 2. For now, let's consider each factor in turn.[1]

B—Blood Flow

Low blood flow in the brain is the number one predictor of future memory problems and Alzheimer's disease and how quickly your brain will deteriorate.[2]

Blood is the channel that supplies cells with nutrients and clears toxins. To keep our brains sharp and healthy for as long as possible, it is critical to protect our blood vessels. In fact, brain cells don't age as quickly as once believed. Research shows it is the blood vessels supporting our neurons that age.[3]

Noting that 20 percent of the body's blood flow is used by the brain, I often tell patients, "Whatever is good for your heart is good for your brain, and whatever is bad for your heart is also bad for your brain." Not only that, but if you have blood flow problems anywhere, you probably have them everywhere.

There are several vascular or blood flow risk factors:

- Cardiovascular disease, including the following:
  - (a) Atherosclerosis (hardening and narrowing of the arteries)
  - (b) High LDL or total cholesterol
  - (c) Heart attack
  - (d) Atrial fibrillation
  - (e) Hypertension or prehypertension
- Erectile dysfunction
- A stroke or transient ischemic attack (TIA)
- Loss-of-oxygen experience (such as near-drowning or heart stoppages)
- Exercising less than twice a week and/or a slow walking speed

Checkup for Blood Flow Issues

BLOOD PRESSURE

Check your blood pressure regularly. The optimal range is 90–120 (systolic), 60–80 (diastolic). Anything above 140 (systolic) or 90 (diastolic) is considered hypertensive. However, blood pressure that is too low (<90 systolic or <60 diastolic) can also be a problem.

LAB TESTS

- **Complete Blood Count (CBC):** This blood test checks the health of your blood, including red and white blood cell counts. A low red blood cell count (anemia) can make you feel anxious and tired and can lead to memory problems. A high level of white blood cells may indicate infection.
- **Lipid Panel:** Cholesterol and triglyceride (fat) levels in the blood are also important, especially because they can negatively affect blood delivery to the brain.

Prescription to Reduce Your Blood Flow Risk

These strategies can help support your overall blood flow and improve your cholesterol levels and blood pressure.

1. **Avoid anything that hurts vascular health.** Examples include a sedentary lifestyle, caffeine, nicotine, and dehydration.

2. **Seek treatment for anything that damages your blood flow.** Be serious about addressing coronary artery disease, heart arrhythmias, prediabetes and diabetes, prehypertension and hypertension, insomnia, sleep apnea, and drug and alcohol abuse.

3. **Lose weight if your BMI is over 25.** BMI, an abbreviation for Body Mass Index, is a measure of body fat based on a person's height and weight. To determine your BMI, check any online BMI calculator.

4. **Spend 10 to 20 minutes a day in deep prayer or meditation.** Both prayer and meditation have been shown to improve blood flow to the brain.

5. **Adopt natural strategies to keep your blood pressure healthy.** There are several options here, including eating more plant-based foods, limiting dairy and salt, drinking water, and getting seven to eight hours of sleep a night.

6. **Take medication if you need it.** I prefer to take a natural approach to health problems,

but hypertension or excessively high cholesterol levels can become a crisis if not managed properly.

7. **Exercise!** Regular exercise helps to boost nitric oxide and keep blood vessels open and flexible.

R—Retirement/Aging

Mental decline is normal with age, but it's not inevitable. Increasing age is the most significant clinical risk factor for memory loss and Alzheimer's disease. Our research shows that most people's brains become less and less active with age. Blood flow drops, and people become much more vulnerable to memory problems, brain fog, and depression.

One of the most exciting lessons I've learned from my years of studying brain scans is that your brain does not have to deteriorate. With a little forethought, you can slow or even reverse the aging process in the brain.

I recently met a woman who told me that now that she was 60 years old, she didn't want to have to worry anymore about what she ate or whether she exercised. She said she was done with that part of her life. If that describes you, I have a question: Are you okay with the consequences of having an older-functioning brain—less energy, brain fog, depression, and bad decisions? As we age, we have less room for error if we want to stay vibrant and healthy. To be at our best and conquer memory loss, we have to be vigilant.

Since the 2008 recession, many people who thought they could retire have had to continue working. The average retirement age rose from 60 to 62. But there can be a silver lining to working longer. A study of nearly 500,000 people found that for each additional year of work, the risk of getting dementia is reduced by 3.2 percent.[4] Working keeps us physically active, socially connected, and mentally stimulated, all of which help prevent cognitive decline. But if your brain is not healthy, you'll have trouble competing against younger talent. Don't let that be you.

Checkup for Retirement/Aging Issues

LAB TESTS

The following tests measure the blood markers of aging and should be part of an annual checkup.

- **C-reactive protein** (CRP) is a measure of inflammation. A healthy range is 0.0 to 1.0 mg/L.
- **Fasting blood sugar and hemoglobin A1C** are two blood tests that screen for prediabetes and diabetes. Age is one of the primary risk factors for both.
- **DHEA (dehydroepiandrosterone)** and **testosterone** are two neurohormones essential to check. DHEA drops with age; higher levels are associated with longevity. Too little testosterone—in both men and women—is associated with depression, poor memory, and low sex drive.
- **Ferritin** blood test measures iron stores. Levels between 50 and 100 ng/mL (nanograms per milliliter) are ideal.

Prescription to Reduce Your Retirement/Aging Risk

1. **Be serious.** After looking at thousands of seniors' brains, I know I'm in a battle for the health of mine. When I don't feel like exercising or eating right, I ask myself, *Which brain*

do you want? An old or a young one? Which do *you* want?

2. **Focus on new learning.** If you want to keep your brain sharp, you must engage in lifelong learning (see chapter 3).

3. **Keep your iron on target.** If your iron level is low, consider taking an iron supplement. If it is too high, you can lower it by donating blood, which benefits you as well as someone else.

4. **Intermittent fasting.** Memory loss is associated with the brain producing too much of certain toxic proteins that damage cells. One way your brain gets rid of these is through intermittent fasting. Think of tiny trash collectors cleaning up the toxins and pieces of dead and diseased cells that gunk up your brain. Nightly 12-to-16-hour fasts have been shown to help.

5. **Get social.** Get involved with your family, church, or other groups. Take a class, form new friendships, share experiences, get physically active, and stay connected with others.

I—Inflammation

Chronic inflammation acts like an ongoing, low-level fire that destroys organs. Just as poor blood flow and oxidative stress can devastate your brain, so can chronic inflammation.

Inflammation is your body's natural way of coping with an injury or infection. It's a vitally important response that must be elicited at the right time and in the right balance. You would never want to completely eliminate inflammation, because your body would not be able to deal with foreign invaders or heal from injuries.

When you are injured or develop an infection, your body's natural defenses jump into action: Blood vessels dilate, blood flow increases to the troubled area, and your immune system's white blood cells (plus substances they produce) rush to deal with the trouble, much like firefighters hurrying to a fire. Nearby areas become swollen, warm, and red as your immune system fights to destroy bacteria and clear the way for healing to begin.

Injury and infection aren't the only things

that trigger or promote inflammation. Others include the following:

- environmental toxins
- smoking
- low levels of vitamin D or omega-3 fatty acids
- hormone imbalances
- gum disease
- gastrointestinal problems ("leaky gut")
- emotional stress
- excess body (especially belly) fat
- high blood sugar levels
- pro-inflammatory foods: sugar and foods that quickly turn to sugar; trans fats; excessive omega-6 fatty acids from vegetable oils

Inflammation that constantly remains on, rather than arising occasionally to heal an injury or infection, is called chronic inflammation. Even though it may operate at a low level, over time, chronic inflammation can damage organs and contribute to a wide range of illnesses, including heart disease, arthritis, gastrointestinal disorders, cancer, Alzheimer's disease, Parkinson's disease, depression, and chronic pain.

Checkup for Inflammation Issues

LAB TESTS

Testing amounts of the following substances in your blood will help you and your doctor determine the level of inflammation in your body and provide direction on what to do about it.

- **C-reactive protein** (CRP) measures inflammation. The most common cause of elevated C-reactive protein is metabolic syndrome or insulin resistance. The second most common cause is sensitivity to food, such as gluten.
- **Interleukin 6** (IL-6) is another measure of inflammation. An elevated amount of IL-6 may mean an inflammatory condition is present, such as an infection or an autoimmune disorder.
- **Homocysteine** is an amino acid that, when elevated, is associated with inflammation, atherosclerosis (hardening and narrowing of

the arteries), and an increased risk of heart attack, stroke, blood clots, and possibly Alzheimer's disease.

- **Folate** aids in the production of DNA and other genetic material. It is required for the healthy regulation of our genes. Folate works together with vitamins B_6 and B_{12} and other nutrients to control blood levels of homocysteine.
- **Vitamin B_{12}** is critically important for healthy brain function. Vitamin B_{12} deficiency can potentially cause severe and irreversible damage, especially to the brain and nervous system. Symptoms such as fatigue, depression, and poor memory can occur at levels only slightly lower than normal.
- **The Omega-3 Index** measures the total amount of omega-3 fatty acids EPA and DHA in red blood cells, which directly reflects their levels in the brain. A low Omega-3 Index increases the risk of cognitive decline by as much as 77 percent.[5]

Prescription to Reduce Your Inflammation Risk

1. **Address the health of your gut.** The gut—your gastrointestinal (GI) tract—is often called the second brain because it is loaded with nerve tissue. It is in direct communication with your brain, which is why you get butterflies when you're excited or have loose bowels when you're upset. Anxiety, depression, stress, and grief all express themselves as emotional pain and, quite often, GI distress. So avoid anything that hurts your gut!

2. **Reduce homocysteine.** B vitamins, especially B_6, B_{12}, and folate, help lower high levels of homocysteine, and they also support brain health.

3. **Boost your omega-3s.** The omega-3 fatty acids EPA and DHA can increase blood flow; slow brain atrophy; increase working memory, executive function, and mood; and decrease inflammation and anxiety.

4. **Take care of your gums.** To decrease inflammation, it is critical to avoid periodontal (gum) disease, a risk factor for dementia.[6]

Brush your teeth twice a day after meals, and floss daily. Flossing your teeth is a brain exercise!

G—Genetics

Humans receive 23 pairs of chromosomes—one set from each parent—that are found in the DNA in the nucleus of cells. Each chromosome contains the genes that provide instruction, or coding, for producing the different kinds of proteins that make up our cells. A healthy person has just the right number of chromosomes and the right number of genes. When the number of chromosomes is wrong, or there are extra or defective genes, health problems occur.

People who have family members with severe memory problems, Alzheimer's disease, or another form of dementia, or those who have one or two copies of the *APOE* e4 gene or several other genes, have a higher risk for memory problems. This is especially true for those with a first-degree relative (mother, father, brother, or sister) with memory issues. They are 3.5 times more likely to develop symptoms. A family history of

Parkinson's disease also makes it more likely that people will develop memory issues.

For the past few decades, scientists have been exploring the new field of *epigenetics*, or the way behaviors, emotions, and environment can turn certain genes on or off. As a result, some illnesses become more or less likely in us as well as in our children, grandchildren, and even great-grandchildren. Geneticists now know that our habits, feelings, and environment affect our biology so deeply that they cause changes in the genes that are transmitted to future generations.

In other words, environmental factors like diet, stress, toxins, and prenatal nutrition can affect the activity of the genes that are passed on to your offspring and beyond.

Checkup for Genetic Issues

KNOW YOUR FAMILY HISTORY

Not everyone has taken the time to find out what happened to their relatives. Reach out to family members so that you can be aware of any branches of your family tree in which memory troubles have appeared.

LAB TEST

- **Apolipoprotein E gene (*APOE*) status:** Everyone has two *APOE* genes, and there are three versions: e2, e3, and e4. As with all genes, we inherit one copy from each parent. A person with one *APOE* e4 gene inherited it from one parent. Someone with two *APOE* e4 genes received one from each parent. A person with one *APOE* e4—or worse, two—has a high chance of experiencing memory problems. This gene increases the chance of developing late-onset Alzheimer's disease by 2.5 times if you have one E4, or 5 to 15 times if you have two e4s.[7] Get tested to know if you carry an *APOE* e4 gene and assess your risk. Any doctor can order this test for you.

Prescription to Reduce Your Genetic Risks

1. **Go for screening early.** For those who have genetic risk factors (a family history of memory problems, dementia, or Alzheimer's), early screening—around age 40—that includes questionnaires, cognitive testing, and possibly brain SPECT (single photon

emission computed tomography) imaging (see page 150) is important. Early screening gives you a window in which to address the other risk factors.

2. **Take your brain health seriously.** If you suspect you have a genetic predisposition to memory issues, caring for your brain is critical.
3. **Hop on the exercise bandwagon.** All of us should exercise, engage in new learning, and take care of our blood vessels, but it is even more imperative if you have genetic risk factors.
4. **Avoid head trauma.** To protect your head from injuries and concussions, avoid contact sports and falls, which are much more common as you age. Practice balance exercises and strengthen your muscles to keep them in shape.

H—Head Trauma

In multiple studies, having one or more head injuries has been associated with an increased risk of lasting memory issues.[8] If the injury occurred before the age of 25, a person has two and a half times the risk of memory problems; if it occurred after 55, a person has almost four times the risk.

Many people think of the brain as firm, fixed, and rubbery, but it's not. It only becomes that way after someone dies and the brain is fixed in formaldehyde. During life, the brain has the consistency of soft butter, tofu, or custard—something between egg whites and Jell-O.[9]

Your very soft brain is housed in a really hard skull that has multiple sharp, bony ridges, which means that the brain is easily damaged. Whiplash, jarring motions (think shaken baby syndrome), blast injuries, and blows to the head can cause the brain to slam into the hard interior ridges of the skull. Each year, about two million new traumatic brain injuries occur.

In addition, because your pituitary gland (the master hormone regulator) sits in a vulnerable part of your skull, it is often damaged in head injuries, causing significant hormonal imbalances.

This is worth repeating over and over: Protect your head. It contains your brain, which runs everything in your life. Seems obvious, right? Yet until very recently, this simple concept escaped the consciousness of many people in our society, me included. We let little children hit soccer balls with their heads and do dangerous gymnastic routines. People cheer at high school football games when the opposing quarterback is knocked out of the action after a vicious hit to his head.

Traumatic brain injuries—even those considered mild without a loss of consciousness and that occurred decades earlier—cause lasting damage that we can clearly see on brain scans. Those injured areas wreak havoc on people's lives, causing depression, suicidal thoughts, panic attacks, temper problems, addictions, and memory and learning issues.

Checkup for Head Trauma Issues

KNOW IF YOU HAVE HAD A CONCUSSION

Take some time to remember whether you ever sustained a concussion or a blow without a concussion (subconcussive impact). Think back (or ask your parents). Did you ever

fall out of a tree or down stairs?
fall off a horse or roof?

dive into a shallow pool?
fall off a fence headfirst?
have a car accident (as a driver or passenger)?
have whiplash?
sustain a work-related head injury?
suffer a concussion or head injury playing sports?

CONSIDER GETTING A FUNCTIONAL IMAGING STUDY

A functional imaging study, such as SPECT (single photon emission computed tomography) or QEEG (quantitative electroencephalogram), may help pinpoint injured areas and is worth investigating if your memory is not what you want it to be or if you have signs of cognitive impairment.

CHECK FOR LOSS OF SMELL (ANOSMIA)

Loss of smell, or anosmia, is a common consequence of head trauma, and it could indicate a serious problem. The olfactory cortex, the area of your brain involved with your sense of smell, is near your memory centers, and these regions tend to deteriorate and die together.

LAB TESTS

Be sure to assess all the other BRIGHT MINDS risk factors that pertain to you, especially through these blood tests:

- **Omega-3 Index:** Brains with a higher index heal better.
- **HbA1c and fasting blood sugar:** Higher levels impair healing.
- **Thyroid, DHEA, and testosterone levels:** Because of where it sits in the skull, the pituitary gland (the master hormone gland) is often damaged when the brain is injured. Testing and treating any hormone deficiencies is important to help heal from traumatic brain injuries.

Prescription to Reduce Your Head Trauma Risk

1. **Reduce your risk of head injury.** Protect your head, wear your seat belt, and avoid high-risk activities if you care about your quality of life. Sports such as football, hockey, soccer, horseback riding, auto racing, and skiing can be dangerous.

2. **Go and smell the roses.** I mean that literally. There is evidence that repeated exposure to certain odors can improve one's ability to smell.[10]

T—Toxins

As a classically trained psychiatrist, I received virtually no training on the impact of toxins on the brain. It wasn't until I started looking at the brain that I started to realize the connection between toxins and health problems.

Research now shows that many people with allergies, autoimmune diseases, neurodegenerative diseases, diabetes, and cancers have one thing in common: exposure to environmental toxins. Our bodies have systems in place to get rid of toxins (through the gut, liver, kidneys, and skin), but when our detoxification systems are overwhelmed, we experience brain fog, fatigue, and life-threatening illnesses. Toxins in any form damage the brain and increase the risk of memory problems and dementia.

Check these lists of common toxins to see which toxic substances you may have been exposed to, either now or in the past.

Toxins that can be ingested or absorbed

- Polluted or tainted water (including lead and arsenic)
- BPA (bisphenol A, found in plastics, food and drink containers, dental sealants, and the coating of cash register receipts)
- PCBs
- Heavy metals, such as mercury, lead, or cadmium
- Excessive alcohol
- Marijuana
- Many medications, such as benzodiazepines (for anxiety or insomnia) or narcotic pain medications
- Chemotherapy
- General anesthesia in some patients
- Silicone breast implants that have leaked
- MSG
- Artificial food dyes, preservatives, and sweeteners
- Herbicides and pesticides
- Foods manufactured with plastic equipment
- Health and beauty products absorbed through the skin

Toxins that can be inhaled

- Air pollution
- Cigarette smoke, secondhand smoke, marijuana smoke
- Automobile exhaust
- Gasoline fumes
- Toxins in the air near high-traffic areas
- Cleaning chemicals
- Welding or soldering fumes
- Fire-retardant fumes
- Carbon monoxide
- Asbestos
- Aviation fumes
- Fireplace fumes
- Paint and solvent fumes
- Pesticide or herbicide residues
- Mold

Because toxins can affect so many parts of the body, they are associated with a wide range of symptoms. Those that are more directly associated with the brain include poor memory and concentration, word confusion, mood issues, headaches, vertigo, and cravings. Other problems range from abdominal pain, diarrhea, smelly stools, bad breath, low appetite, and weight issues to skin rashes, fatigue and weakness, aches and muscle cramps, numbness and tingling, tremors, sweats, and problems with temperature regulation.

Checkup for Toxin Issues

LAB TESTS

Your liver has a finite toxin-processing capacity; therefore, it is highly vulnerable to toxic overload. The following tests can help determine how strained it is.

Liver function

- **ALT (SGPT):** Normal range: 7 to 56 units per liter (U/L)
- **AST (SGOT):** Normal range: 5 to 40 U/L
- **Bilirubin:** Normal range: 0.2 to 1.2 mg/dL
- **Zinc:** Normal range: 60 to 110 μg/dL (low zinc will limit detoxification in the liver)

If your liver function tests are high, cut back on your intake of sugar, simple carbohydrates, and alcohol. Also, you and your doctor might consider whether hepatitis or medications that raise liver enzymes, such as acetaminophen (Tylenol), could be affecting your liver's function.

Kidney function

- **BUN 7:** Normal range: 20 mg/dL
- **Creatinine:** Normal range: 0.5 to 1.2 mg/dL

Skin

- **Check for rashes, acne, and rosacea.** All are clues to detoxification problems.

Prescription to Reduce Your Toxin Risk

1. **Limit your exposure to toxins.** Do the following:

   » *Quit smoking.*

   » *Address drug and/or alcohol abuse.*

   » *Slowly replace "silver" dental fillings.*

   » *Reduce your consumption of toxin-contaminated foods* by buying organic.

   » *Buy and store foods in glass jars* when possible.

   » *Avoid processed meats* (which contain

nitrosamines and cause the liver to produce fats that are toxic to the brain).

- *Add fiber and fiber-rich foods.*
- *Drink three to four quarts of clean water a day.*
- *Do a food detox.* For two weeks, eliminate processed foods, gluten, dairy, non-organic beef and chicken, farmed fish, the "Dirty Dozen" produce items (see https://www.ewg.org/foodnews/summary.php), soy, artificial sweeteners, alcohol and recreational drugs, and nonpurified water.
- *Check your home for mold, and change the filters on your heating and cooling system regularly.*
- *Decrease your use of unsafe health and beauty aids.*
- *Clean the house thoroughly.*

2. **Strengthen your detoxification systems.** Support your gut, support your skin, and work up a sweat with exercise. Sweating is one of the best natural ways to cleanse your system.

M—Mental Health Issues

Getting your mind right is a critical piece of the puzzle in rescuing and strengthening your memory. Studies have shown that untreated depression, bipolar disorder, schizophrenia, post-traumatic stress disorder (PTSD), ADD/ADHD, and chronic stress significantly increase the risk of memory problems, inflammation, and vascular and immunity issues. Poor mental health can be very potent. In fact, new research indicates that men who are depressed are at greater risk of suffering a heart attack or heart disease than men who are obese, and people with mental health issues die an average of 10 years earlier than their mentally healthy counterparts.[11]

Anything that negatively affects your mind also negatively affects your brain. Virtually all psychiatric illnesses have a significant brain component to them.

For example, chronic stress in midlife has been associated with memory problems later on. Brain circuits involved in chronic anxiety and fear extensively overlap in areas associated with Alzheimer's disease, and chronic stress has been shown to decrease the size of the hippocampus and prefrontal cortex. Stress is considered a normal part of life when it is occasional and temporary, such as when you feel anxious before an exam or a job interview. When it becomes frequent or chronic, as in prolonged grief, however, it needs to be treated.

Checkup for Mental Health Issues

SCREEN FOR PROBLEMS

Given that ADHD, PTSD, depression, bipolar disorder, schizophrenia, and chronic stress are risk factors for memory problems as we age, it is important to screen for them. You can visit www.amenclinics.com to determine whether you have the common symptoms of ADHD, depression, bipolar disorder, and PTSD and should seek further help.

Prescription for Reducing Your Mental Health Risk

1. **Get treated.** Early treatment is essential to stave off the ravages of psychiatric illnesses. With appropriate treatment, the brain becomes more balanced and works much more efficiently. Work with a skilled mental

health professional—your brain depends on it.

2. **Try these research-proven tips.** Use them to lower stress and boost your level of happiness and overall mental health.

    - Start every day with the words "Today is going to be a great day." Your mind makes happen what it visualizes.
    - Write down the name of one person you appreciate every day. Then tell him or her. Appreciation builds positive bridges between people.
    - Pray about your concerns. When you pray, you turn over your worries to God, who is sovereign, loving, and active in our lives: "Give all your worries and cares to God, for he cares about you" (1 Peter 5:7).
    - Limit screen time. Studies report higher levels of depression and obesity with increased time spent with technology.
    - Exercise. It is the fastest way to feel better.

- Enjoy some dark chocolate. It can boost blood flow to your brain, improve your mood, and decrease anxiety.
- Listen to music. Just 25 minutes of Mozart or Strauss has been shown to lower blood pressure and stress.
- Choose experiences that give you a sense of awe, such as looking at a sunset or something beautiful in nature.
- Drink green tea, which contains L-theanine, an ingredient that helps you feel happier, more relaxed, and more focused.
- Read an inspiring, powerful novel.
- Stop complaining! It rewires your brain to see the negative far too often.
- Do something you love that brings you joy.
- Engage in activities that make you feel competent.
- Learn to forgive. It can reduce negative feelings.
- Help someone else or volunteer. Make time for friends, too.
- Journal your feelings. Not only does it

get them out of your head, it helps you gain perspective.

» Learn to kill the ANTs (automatic negative thoughts). Remember that thoughts aren't necessarily accurate. Whenever you feel sad, mad, nervous, or out of control, write down your negative thoughts. Next, ask yourself if they are true or if they are distorted to make you feel worse. Focusing your mind on positive, rational thoughts will help you feel much better.

I—Immunity/Infection Issues

It is important to constantly strengthen and build up your immunity. Consider the infamous December 1981 trash collectors' strike in New York City. Suddenly, the city's rats got to join in the Christmas spirit with plentiful meals on the sidewalks. But not everyone was as happy as the rodents. Tempers flared. Where did the vermin come from? It turns out they were always there, but when the streets were swept clean of junk, the rats were kept under control. They stayed hidden because there was nothing in plain sight to eat. During the sanitation department's strike, however, garbage was everywhere, so the rats wound up running rampant, multiplying and spreading disease. So, too, when you put trash in your body or don't regularly keep your immune system healthy, you become vulnerable to "vermin": serious illnesses, immune dysfunction, and brain disease.

Immunity is your body's natural defense system. In a general sense, it has two broad duties: *defense* and *tolerance*. For the first, it helps to defend against invaders from outside your body, such as bacteria, viruses, and parasites. Your immune system also patrols your body, looking for troublemakers, such as cancer cells. Second, the immune system helps determine your tolerance of potential triggers from the outside world, such as allergens, as well as internal attacks, such as autoimmune disorders.

When your defenses break down, you are more vulnerable to infections and cancer. When your body's tolerance is overwhelmed, you have more issues with allergies and autoimmune disorders, in which your body attacks itself. Both autoimmune disorders and infections (especially when they become chronic) increase your risk of brain fog, memory issues, and dementia.

Checkup for Immunity or Infectious Disease Issues

KNOW YOUR PERSONAL HISTORY

If you have a history of allergies, rashes, or repeated infections, it could indicate an immune system vulnerability.

LAB TESTS

The following blood tests are important to determine the health of your immune system.

- **Complete blood count with differential** to look at the distribution of white blood cells, one of the principal actors of the immune system.
- **Erythrocyte sedimentation rate (ESR):** This common test is a nonspecific measure of inflammation, which is high in autoimmune disorders.
- **Antinuclear antibodies (ANA):** The immune system normally makes antibodies to

help fight infection, but antinuclear antibodies often attack the body's own tissues. Test results are often high in autoimmune disorders.

- **Rheumatoid factor (Rh):** Rh is an antibody measurable in the blood. It can bind to other antibodies and cause problems.
- **Vitamin D:** The liver and kidneys convert vitamin D into a hormone that regulates almost all organs. The blood test to get: 25-hydroxyvitamin D level. A normal level is 30 to 100 ng/mL; an optimal level is 50 to 100 ng/mL.

Prescription to Reduce Your Immunity and Infectious Disease Risk

1. **Work with a knowledgeable health-care professional.** You need a medical partner to diagnose and treat any immune system issues or infections.
2. **Do an elimination diet for a month.** Try staying away from sugar, gluten, dairy, corn,

soy, artificial colors, additives, and preservatives to see if you feel better.

3. **Optimize your vitamin D level.** Vitamin D is essential for brain health, mood, memory, and weight control.

4. **Work on managing stress.** Stress lowers immunity and increases the risk of autoimmune diseases.

N—Neurohormone Deficiencies

When your brain, adrenal glands, sex organs, pancreas, and thyroid gland work together, they produce just the right amounts of hormones: chemical messengers that control many of the body's basic functions. This symphony of hormones can be affected by many factors, both inside and outside your body. When they are working in concert, you feel great. When any of these organs is out of sync, however, you can feel awful. Problems start when too much or not enough of one hormone (or several) is produced, which can throw off the delicate balance.

You can experience two types of problems when your hormones are out of balance:

1. Uncomfortable symptoms that can change how you think, feel, and act, affecting your quality of life
2. An increased risk of illness, such as depression, Alzheimer's, heart disease, osteoporosis, diabetes, and certain cancers

Communication between hormones and the brain is strongly two-way: The brain produces signals that trigger the release of hormones, and hormones from other parts of the body also influence the brain.

Checkup for Neurohormone Issues

LAB TESTS

After age 40, be sure to undergo yearly testing of the following hormones for men and women. Note that each lab determines what readings fall in the normal range, so ask for a lab's standards if they don't provide them.

- **Thyroid panel (blood test):**
  - *Hormones:* The thyroid produces three main thyroid hormones: TSH, T3, and T4. These hormones are among the most influential in your body, and all have to be in the right balance to keep your brain and body healthy.
    - *TSH:* Anything over 3.0 is abnormal and needs further investigation.
    - *Free T3:* Active thyroid.
    - *Free T4:* Inactive thyroid.
  - *Thyroid antibodies*
    - thyroid peroxidase (TPO) antibodies.
    - thyroglobulin antibodies (TG).
- **Liver function tests:** Ninety-five percent of T4 is "activated" in the liver, so having a healthy liver is essential.
- **Ferritin level:** Ferritin is like the bus that drives active T3 into the cells; ferritin needs to be above 50 for this to occur.
- **Cortisol (saliva):** Cortisol and DHEA (dehydroepiandrosterone) are produced by the adrenals and are critically involved in your

body's reaction to stress. The cortisol test is best done four times, at intervals throughout the day (to track your daily cycle): when you first wake up, around lunchtime, around dinnertime, and just before you go to sleep. Ideally, your cortisol levels are high in the morning (to wake you up) and taper off slowly during the day and evening, allowing you to fall into a restful sleep at night.

- **DHEA-S (blood test):** Normal blood levels of DHEA-sulfate can differ by sex and age.
- **Free and total serum testosterone (blood test):** Having an optimal level of testosterone is important for your health and well-being. Too much can cause behavioral problems, such as aggression, but too little is associated with depression, poor memory, and low libido.
- **Estrogen and progesterone for women:** These levels can be measured in blood or saliva. Women who have menstrual periods are usually tested on day 21 of their cycle;

postmenopausal women can be measured anytime.

Prescription to Reduce Your Neurohormone Risk

1. **Love your hormones.** To have a great brain, you have to care about the health of your hormones. Make optimizing them a priority, and your life will be much happier.

2. **Limit the bad; expand the good.** To keep your hormones healthy, it is critical to avoid or limit anything that hurts or diminishes them, including smoking, stress, processed food, too much sugar, high amounts of unhealthy fats, wheat, lack of sleep, excessive caffeine, more than a few glasses of alcohol a week, and obesity. To expand the good, exercise, lift weights, get adequate sleep, eat a healthy diet, and manage your stress.

3. **Steer clear of endocrine disrupters.** Pesticides are known to cause hormonal imbalances, and some pesticides have been shown to act as endocrine disrupters, interfering with the

body's natural hormone systems and causing an array of health problems.

4. **Use hormone supplements and medications wisely.** Use bioidentical hormones when possible, as they mimic the molecular structure of the hormones your body makes. Bioidenticals generally have fewer side effects.

D—Diabesity

Diabetes develops when insulin, the hormone that regulates blood sugar levels, becomes deficient or ineffective. The illness has two forms: Type 1 diabetes occurs when the body refuses to make insulin, and type 2 develops when the body mismanages it. In both types, the body is subjected to chronically high blood sugar levels, which damage blood vessels, causing them to become brittle, inflexible, and more likely to break. Damaged blood vessels cannot supply nutrients or take away toxins, which ultimately leads to problems with every organ in the body, including the brain.

Risk factors for diabetes include aging, a family history of the disease, excessive consumption of sugar and high-glycemic foods, obesity, alcohol abuse, exposure to toxins, and a sedentary lifestyle. Watch for these warning signs: increased urination, excessive thirst, increased appetite, and delayed wound healing.

The negative effects of diabetes include increased inflammation, depression, Alzheimer's disease and vascular dementia, strokes, heart disease, hypertension, and accelerated aging. Diabetes has been linked to decreased blood flow to the brain (the number one predictor of future memory problems) and a smaller hippocampus. Scientists have been studying whether medications for diabetes might help people with Alzheimer's, and the answer seems to be yes.

Even mildly elevated blood sugar levels and prediabetes are significant problems and are associated with brain atrophy, memory problems, and dementia.[12] The higher your blood sugar level, the higher your odds of getting dementia.

Here is the scariest part of this story: Diabetes and prediabetes now affect a horrifying 50 percent of the US population.[13] Our sedentary lifestyles and standard American diet (SAD), along with increased toxins, are likely to blame. The great news is that a majority of these cases are preventable. Lifestyle changes have actually been shown to reverse the disease.

Checkup for Diabesity Issues

To make sure your weight doesn't become a health issue, you should always know how you stack up on these health numbers.

BODY MASS INDEX (BMI)

Your BMI is a measure of weight compared to height. An optimal BMI is between 18.5 and 25; the overweight category falls between 25 and 30; over 30 indicates obesity, and over 40 indicates morbid obesity.

LAB TESTS

Get blood tests for your fasting blood sugar, insulin, and hemoglobin every year. If they are abnormal, think of it as a health crisis to be taken very seriously.

Prescription to Reduce Your Diabesity Risk

The exciting news about diabesity is that, with a targeted plan, you can significantly decrease your odds of diabetes and related illness. As with all the BRIGHT MINDS risk factors, it is important to take the long view and develop a lifestyle you can live with and feel happy about.

1. **Follow the Memory Rescue Diet.** It's especially important to limit high-glycemic, low-fiber foods (sugar and foods that turn to sugar), wheat (including whole wheat), and processed foods, and to eat a diet high in smart carbohydrates, which are high in fiber and low on the glycemic index. This diet will give the pancreas a break from constantly having to secrete high levels of insulin and will make your cells more insulin-sensitive. See chapter 2 for the details of this diet.
2. **Lose weight slowly (if you need to lose).** It's the healthiest way to drop pounds and keep

them off. A good, safe rule of thumb is one to two pounds a week. Here are some weight-loss tips:

- Drink more water.
- Have protein for breakfast to balance your blood sugar.
- Decaffeinated green tea and coffee have been shown to increase metabolism and decrease the risk of diabetes, and both are loaded with antioxidants. Be careful, though, what you put in them.
- Cook with coconut oil.
- Don't drink your calories. The calories you drink are more quickly absorbed than those you have to chew.
- Find a healthy plan to guide you in healthy food choices for the rest of your life—like the Memory Rescue Diet (see chapter 2).
- Take saunas and eat detoxifying foods.
- Don't overdo your weight loss. Being too thin is not the answer. A too-low BMI is associated with cognitive problems.[14]

3. **Exercise!** It's known to improve blood sugar levels and reduce weight, and it also helps with detoxification. Strength training has been shown to be particularly effective.

4. **Check with your physician to see if other treatment is necessary.** Depending on your personal numbers and your genetic risks, you may be able to improve your health without resorting to medication.

S—Sleep Issues

A number of studies link sleep problems, such as insomnia and sleep apnea, to a higher risk of memory problems and dementia. But effectively treating these disorders can have a positive impact on memory and brain function.[15]

Proper sleep is essential for brain health. In fascinating new research, scientists have shown that your brain cleanses or "washes" itself during sleep. The brain has a special waste management system that helps get rid of toxins that build up over the course of a day, including the beta-amyloid plaques associated with Alzheimer's disease. Your brain is so busy managing your life during the daylight hours that this cleaning system is pretty much turned off. One theory about why people with dementia sleep so much is that their brains are trying to clear out the accumulating plaques/gunk.

Without healthy sleep, the brain's cleaning crew does not have enough time to do its job, and trash builds up, causing brain fog and memory problems. How would your home look if no one cleaned it for a month? That is the effect chronic insomnia can have on your brain, and unfortunately, it is all too common.

Many lifestyle habits, illnesses, and stresses can trigger insomnia, including poor sleep hygiene, depression, worry, restless leg syndrome, hormonal imbalances (especially progesterone in women), and shift work.

Researchers suggest we aim for seven to eight hours of sleep a night.

Checkup for Sleep Issues

GET ASSESSED FOR SLEEP APNEA

If you snore loudly, stop breathing at night, or are chronically tired during the day, get evaluated at a sleep laboratory, or have your health-care professional order a home sleep apnea study.

DETERMINE THE NUMBER OF HOURS OF SLEEP YOU NEED EACH NIGHT

One way to do this: Whenever you are free to experiment (say, on vacation), go to bed at the same time each night without setting an alarm, and see what time you awaken the next morning. Over a week or 10 days' time, you will discover what your natural sleep needs are. If you are unable to try this, strive to get seven to eight hours each night, which is a healthy amount for most people.

Prescription to Reduce Your Sleep Risk

1. **Treat sleep apnea.** If you have symptoms of the disorder, discuss it with your doctor. Be serious about treatment if you have it.

2. **Avoid sleep robbers.** Negative emotions, medication side effects, and a poor sleep environment can be culprits, as can gadgets close to the bed and drinking caffeine and eating too close to bedtime.

3. **Adopt these sleep enhancers.** To get a better night's sleep and allow your brain time to clean itself up, try one or more of the following ideas.

   - *Set up your bedroom for sleep.* It should be cool, completely dark, and quiet.
   - *Block gadget disruption.* Stash your phone, tablet, and digital watch away from your bed, or at least turn the sound off. Face your digital clock toward the wall.
   - *Ban pets from the bedroom*—or at least keep them off the bed.
   - *Try to fix emotional problems before bedtime.* If you are a worrier, devote about 10 to 15 minutes before bedtime to your nagging concerns; then put a stop to them. If you're at odds with someone, send him or her a positive text or e-mail—or determine to deal with the issue in the morning. Doing so may prevent your anger from festering and growing further. In other words, "don't let the sun go down while you are still angry" (Ephesians 4:26).
   - *Establish and stick to a regular sleep schedule.*

Try to go to bed at the same time each night and wake up at the same time each morning, including on weekends.

- *Read a book before bed.* Preferably, pick up something thick or tedious. Avoid reading from an e-reader or tablet; its light will keep your brain alert.
- *Don't take daytime naps.* Napping is one of the biggest mistakes insomniacs can make, since it compounds the nighttime sleep-cycle disruption.
- *Don't exercise within four hours of bedtime.* Regular workouts are a great way to combat insomnia, but vigorous exercise late in the evening may keep you up.
- *Wear socks to bed.* Warm hands and feet are the best predictors of rapid sleep onset, according to researchers.
- *Cut out caffeinated beverages in the afternoon or evening.* Refrain from drinking coffee, tea, or other caffeinated beverages after 2 p.m.
- *Use the bed and bedroom only for sexual activity or sleep.* Sexual activity releases muscle tension and a flood of natural

hormones. Adults with healthy sex lives tend to sleep better and feel better overall. If you are unable to fall asleep or stay asleep, move to another room.

» *Stay away from benzodiazepines and traditional sleep medications.* When medications are necessary, I often prescribe trazodone, gabapentin, and amitriptyline to my patients.
» *Develop a relaxing nighttime routine that encourages sleep.*

CHAPTER 2

CONSUME THE RIGHT FUEL

CHOOSING THE RIGHT FOODS is one of the most important strategies of all for conquering memory loss. Your brain uses 20 to 30 percent of the calories you consume. It is the most energy-hungry organ in your body. If you eat a fast-food diet, you will have a fast-food mind that is less capable of quick thinking and reliable decision-making.

In this chapter I want to introduce you to a diet that everyone should follow if they want to protect their memory. Once you commit to the brain-healthy diet I discuss, you will quickly notice that you have more energy; fewer cravings; better focus, memory, and moods; and even a flatter stomach within a matter of weeks.

A number of recent studies report that a healthy diet, like the Memory Rescue Diet, is associated with significantly lower risks of severe memory problems, such as Alzheimer's disease, as well as most of the risk factors I've discussed, including heart disease, inflammation, depression, and diabesity.[1] Healthy diets are also associated with bigger brain size.[2] And bigger is better when it comes to the brain.

Over the past three decades I have developed a new approach to diet that focuses on changing the way you think about eating as well as the way you actually eat. These two principles form the backbone of the Memory Rescue Diet. They are designed to guide you to make the best food choices for your brain for the rest of your life. Here's an overview:

1. Change the Way You Think about Eating
   - ☐ Get your mind right.
   - ☐ Think of calories like money: spend them wisely.

- ☐ Beware the standard American diet (SAD).

2. Change the Way You Eat (and Drink)
   - ☐ Pick the healthiest protein.
   - ☐ Get your fill of the right fats.
   - ☐ Go for the greens (and reds, yellows, blues, and other hues).
   - ☐ Choose brain-boosting carbohydrates.
   - ☐ Say good-bye to sugar.
   - ☐ Hydrate with H_2O.
   - ☐ Flavor your food with brain-smart spices and herbs.

As you adopt these healthy eating habits, you will begin developing a new, healthy relationship with food. Contrary to what you might think, eating in a brain-healthy way is not more expensive. It is *less* expensive, when you consider that your medical bills will be lower and your productivity will go up. And what price can you put on your memory?

In fact, the Memory Rescue Diet includes no gimmicks, and there are no "designer" foods to buy. Plus, it is simple. I know you won't follow a program that is complicated or requires you to eat boring foods for the next 40 years. I wouldn't—why would anyone else? The recommended foods are delicious, energizing, and healing.

Change the Way You Think about Eating

Get Your Mind Right

Too many patients I've seen start with this attitude: "I don't want to deprive myself. I want what I want when I want it."

My response is "Which do you want *more*? Your health, a great brain, years added to your life, and freedom from dementia . . . or the nightly alcohol and sugar?"

Most people fail in nutrition programs because they focus on what they cannot have rather than on what they can have. They have a deprivation mind-set. They focus on the loss of the very foods that drive inflammation and hijack their taste buds—empty-calorie, sugary, fast, and pesticide-laden foods.

To rescue your memory, the first thing you must do is get your mind right.

In my experience, as people start down the

road to getting well, they begin to miss the Rocky Road ice cream, look longingly at the doughnuts, and feel sad about not being able to eat the chicken fried steak, mashed potatoes, and key lime pie. Yet after about 10 days of eating high-quality food, they realize that their taste buds have come alive and food tastes better than ever.

Getting well is about focusing on an abundance of the right nutrients, which will deprive you of illnesses like diabetes, heart disease, cancer, depression, and dementia. This is a critical shift. Those who continue to follow the Memory Rescue Diet begin to see many unhealthy foods as weapons of self-destruction and avoid them, just as they would avoid shaking hands with someone who was sneezing and coughing up green gunk.

Think of your relationship with food the way you think about your other relationships. Find foods you love that love you back, and stay away from those that abuse you. Just because you "love" something doesn't mean it's good for you. I had a patient tell me she'd rather get Alzheimer's disease than give up sugar. That is an example of an abusive relationship. She was in love with something that hurt her. Fortunately, over time she ended the toxic relationship and helped her whole family get well.

Think of Calories like Money: Spend Them Wisely

Thoughtful, successful people tend to be conscientious with their money. They save for retirement and spend their hard-earned cash wisely. Those who don't are much more likely to experience financial hardship or to file for bankruptcy. I think of calories the same way. They are incredibly important, and you should spend them carefully. That means using your calories on foods that nourish you rather than on those that steal from your health.

Make no mistake, the quality of your food matters more than the quantity. Compare a 500-calorie blueberry crumb doughnut to a 500-calorie plate of rainbow trout, broccoli, orange bell peppers, raspberries, and almonds. The doughnut will zap your energy and set off an inflammatory response; the fish meal will power your brain and reduce your risk of accelerated aging. You are likely to gulp down the first in a matter of minutes, sending your blood sugar sky-high and teasing your pleasure centers; the second you enjoy at a leisurely pace, and it helps you feel full longer as well as happier and more emotionally stable.

This is not to say that the quantity of calories you take in is unimportant. On the contrary, substantial research, first in animals and now in humans, indicates that a calorie-restricted (CR) diet can help control weight; decrease the risk of heart disease, cancer, and stroke; and trigger mechanisms in the body that increase the production of nerve growth factors, which are helpful to the brain. Eating too many calories causes waste to build up in the body's cells, making everything look and feel older.

However, calorie restriction has drawbacks: It is hard to maintain long-term and has been associated with decreased testosterone levels, irritability, and a lower sex drive. Scientists have looked at other ways to mimic the benefits of CR without these side effects, including the antidiabetic drug metformin, which lowers high blood sugar levels; exercise; stress management; and improved sleep.

There may be another way to keep your calorie intake in check. A possible cause of memory loss is the overproduction of beta-amyloid and abnormal tau proteins that damage brain cell circuits. One way your brain eliminates these proteins is through autophagy,[3] a process that's like having tiny trash collectors cleaning up the toxins. Nightly 12- to 16-hour fasts turn on this process. That means if you eat dinner at 7 p.m. and don't eat again until between 7 and 11 a.m., you give your brain time for trash cleanup. This "intermittent fasting," as it is called, can significantly improve memory, mood, fat loss, weight, blood pressure, and inflammatory markers. You can also use this method of eating to reduce your calorie consumption—for example, by skipping breakfast and eating only lunch and dinner two or three days each week.

New research also suggests that you should avoid eating within two to three hours of bedtime[4] and that late-night eating puts you at a higher risk of heart attack and stroke. Eating late puts your brain in a "high alert" stress state, causing your body to release stress hormones when it should be winding down. In healthy people, blood pressure drops by at least 10 percent when they sleep, but late-night eaters' blood pressure stays high. People whose blood pressure does not fall at night are known as "nondippers," and they have a much higher rate of heart-related death. Research has shown that late eaters are nearly three times more likely to be nondippers. You don't want to be one of them.

Two things seem certain: Consuming too many calories is bad for your brain and body, and if you are going to put something into your body, you want to be sure you are getting the biggest health bang for the cost.

Beware the Standard American Diet (SAD)

No one makes a *conscious* decision to eat foods that trigger inflammation, but that is exactly what most Americans do in consuming the standard American diet of fast food, sugar, simple carbohydrates, dairy products, trans fats, some animal-derived saturated fats, excess omega-6 fatty acids, nutrient-bankrupt refined and processed foods, and products filled with pesticide residues, antibiotics, and hormones. This type of diet is loaded with chemicals that are unnatural to your body, which causes it to respond as if it has been injured. Inflammation is your body and brain's healing response to that injury. Over time, if your diet doesn't change, the inflammation can become chronic, and as we've seen, that can lead to many health problems. It's enough to make anyone feel *SAD*!

Right now, make a commitment to becoming more aware of and serious about the foods you put in your body. Aim to eat "clean" foods that are organically grown or raised and free of hormones, antibiotics, and pesticides. Whenever possible, choose meat from animals that are free range and/or grass fed, and organically grown nuts and seeds. Start reading food labels, and do your best to avoid food additives and artificial preservatives, dyes, and sweeteners.

Organic and sustainably raised produce can be pricey, so it helps to know which fruits and vegetables carry the highest pesticide loads and to buy organic when it matters most. I consult the Environmental Working Group's annual lists of foods with the highest and lowest levels of pesticide residues and recommend that you do so as well. (Stay updated at www.ewg.org.) Try to buy organic when purchasing the fruits and vegetables on these lists.

Change the Way You Eat (and Drink)

Pick the Healthiest Protein

It may come as a surprise to learn that the only component of your body more abundant than water is protein. You need protein to keep your cells, tissues, and organs growing and functioning properly. It also contributes to the health of everything from your muscles, hair, and skin to various hormones and neurotransmitters, which all require a steady supply of the 20 amino acids that are the building blocks of protein. A portion of these amino acids are made by your body, but the rest must come from the food you eat.

Protein is also a critical part of your diet because of its role in maintaining a healthy metabolism. It stimulates the release of metabolic hormones that help stabilize your blood sugar levels and stop energy crashes. As a result, eating or snacking on protein helps you feel full longer than you do after a high-carb or sugary snack or meal. And because protein takes more energy to digest, you also wind up burning more calories.

With all these benefits, you might think you

need to eat lots of protein to stay healthy, but small quantities are all that is required. In fact, consuming too much can be detrimental, as it accelerates the internal processes (oxidation, inflammation) that contribute to faster aging and disease. Our recommendation at Amen Clinics is to eat a limited amount with every meal, and snack every four to five hours to help balance your blood sugar and decrease cravings.

Given that small doses are better for you than large ones, it becomes even more important to choose the highest-quality protein. High-quality animal protein, whether lamb, turkey, chicken, beef, or pork, is free of hormones and antibiotics, free range, and grass fed. Though it is more expensive than industrial farm-raised animal protein, it is a good investment in your health. Compared with grass-fed meat, industrially raised meat is about 30 percent higher in palmitic acid (a type of unhealthy saturated fat), which has been linked with cardiovascular disease. And don't forget fish, beans and other legumes, raw unsalted nuts, and high-protein veggies, such as broccoli and spinach. Fish, poultry, and most meats contain *all* the necessary amino acids, while plant foods contain only *some* of them. However, plant foods are an essential part of a healthy diet—not just for their protein but also for their many disease-preventing phytonutrients.

Get Your Fill of the Right Fats

Healthy fats are essential to keeping your body and brain disease-free. A case in point: A Mayo Clinic study found that the risk of Alzheimer's disease was 42 percent lower in people who ate a fat-based diet; 21 percent lower in those who ate a protein-based diet; and *400 percent higher* in those who ate a simple carbohydrate–based diet (think bread, pasta, potatoes, rice, and sugar).[5] It's the sugar, *not* the fat, that's the problem.

The war on fat is over—at least in terms of dietary fat. It is clear that your body needs good fats for a variety of essential functions, from storing energy and maintaining healthy brain function to creating healthy cells and hormones. Eating more of the right fats will also help you lose body fat. Research has shown that eating a moderate-fat versus a low-fat diet (35 versus 20 percent of calories from fat) can mean the difference between losing weight and waistline inches and actually *gaining* both! A moderate-fat diet has another advantage: Healthy fats help with satiety—feeling full. In the study mentioned above, 54 percent of the moderate-fat dieters were able to follow their program for the entire 18 months, while only 20 percent of the low-fat dieters were able to stick with theirs.

Notice that I keep reiterating the terms *good* and *healthy* when describing the fats you should be eating. You still need to avoid the so-called bad fats: fried fats, trans fats, and some saturated fats. Here is a look at how different kinds of fats impact your health.

Unsaturated fats. These are beneficial fats, thanks to their role in improving cholesterol levels, easing inflammation, stabilizing heart rhythms, and balancing blood sugar. There are two kinds of unsaturated fats: *polyunsaturated fatty acids* and *monounsaturated fatty acids* (commonly referred to as PUFAs and MUFAs). Unsaturated fats are predominantly found in plant foods, such as vegetable oils (like olive oil), nuts, and seeds. There are two important polyunsaturated fats:

- *Omega-3 fatty acids.* Two types of omega-3s in particular, EPA and DHA, are crucial for optimal brain health and are found in cold-water fish, such as salmon, mackerel, sardines, and trout. Getting inadequate amounts of EPA and DHA (which must come from your diet) puts you at greater risk of cognitive decline in aging, psychological disturbances, depression, and many other illnesses. Higher levels of EPA and DHA are associated with significantly less beta-amyloid in the blood, a reduced incidence of Alzheimer's, and slower cognitive decline.[6]
- *Omega-6 fatty acids*, like omega-3s, are essential for health, playing a critical role in brain function as well as in normal growth and development. Sources include most vegetable oils (soybean, sunflower, safflower, corn, canola), many fried foods, cereals, whole-grain breads, and processed foods. However, overconsumption of omega-6 fatty acids can cancel out the benefits of omega-3s, and the standard American diet, with its overabundance of

omega-6-rich vegetable oils, puts many people's ratio of omega-6s to omega-3s at a whopping 20 to 1 or even higher (an optimal ratio may be less than 4 to 1). This high ratio is pro-inflammatory and increases the risk of heart disease, cancer, diabetes, and many other health problems.

To reach a more favorable balance of omega-6s to omega-3s, eat fewer foods that contain omega-6s and more with omega-3 EPA and DHA. Taking fish oil supplements can also help maintain a healthy omega balance.

Saturated fats. These fats can be either bad *or* good, depending on their structure. Here are a few examples of potentially healthy and unhealthy saturated fatty acids:

» *Butyric acids* are found in fiber-rich foods like sweet potatoes, vegetables, beans, nuts, and fruit, as well as in butter and ghee (clarified butter).
» *Caprylic*, *capric*, and *lauric acids* are found in coconut and, although saturated, can

be used by the brain to make energy and have shown memory benefits, particularly in people with blood sugar problems.[7]

- *Myristic acid* is found in most animal fats (including dairy foods) and some vegetable oils. These fatty acids may be detrimental to heart health, so they should be consumed only in small amounts.
- *Palmitic acid* negatively affects cholesterol and heart health. This fat is created in your liver when you eat a high-sugar, high-carbohydrate diet. It also creates the marbling in the meat of corn-fed cattle.
- *Stearic acid* is found in grain-fed meats, sausage and bacon, cold cuts, peanuts, peanut butter, margarine, fried potatoes, whole milk, cheese, and vegetable oils (it is highest in sunflower oil). Although chocolate is high in stearic acid, it is also high in antioxidants and flavonoids, which help balance its health benefits when eaten in small amounts.

Overall, the healthiest strategy is to cut back on saturated fats like myristic, palmitic, and stearic acids and add more polyunsaturated fats (fish oil, nuts, and seeds) to your diet.

Trans fats. These synthetic fats, or "Frankenfats," are the *worst* fats. They have no place in your diet. They are associated with memory problems, even in young adults.[8] They also decrease healthy blood flow and increase the likelihood of clots, which can cause strokes and heart disease. Partially hydrogenated vegetable oils, shortening, margarine, many processed foods, commercially prepared fried foods, and packaged baked goods, including doughnuts, crackers, and snack foods, contain trans fats.

Go for the Greens (and Reds, Yellows, Blues, and Other Hues)

If you were to do nothing else to change your diet except eat more colorful fruits and vegetables, you would still get enormous benefits from the nutrients, vitamins, and minerals they contain, which your body needs for robust health. Broccoli and other cruciferous vegetables, for example, as well as various herbs and spices (e.g., curcumin) contain sulforaphane, which powerfully assists in DNA repair. Foods from plants of every color, even white, also help prevent cancer and reduce the inflammation that contributes to Alzheimer's disease, heart disease, arthritis, gastrointestinal disorders, and many other illnesses. Plant nutrients bolster your immune system in its role of fending off attacks and disease. (Just be sure to eat twice as many vegetables as fruits to avoid the extra sugar.)

Some of the most age-defying ingredients in produce are its antioxidants, which decrease the destruction caused by free radicals in the body. Blueberries have a well-deserved reputation for being a brain-healthy food, but acai fruit and raspberries have even more antioxidant clout. And a number of herbs and spices—cloves, oregano, rosemary, thyme, cinnamon, turmeric, and sage—have true antioxidant superpowers.

Choose Brain-Boosting Carbohydrates

It makes perfect sense to discuss the best carbohydrates for your brain right after touting the benefits of fruits and vegetables because some of the healthiest carbs are . . . fruits and vegetables!

Veggies like brussels sprouts and asparagus, which are nonstarchy, and fruits like pears and apples are complex carbohydrates, the best kinds of carbs to eat as they are high in fiber, slower to digest, and low glycemic (which means they don't cause your blood sugar to shoot up). If you can swap foods like these for the high-glycemic, low-fiber carbs in your diet—the doughnuts, pizza, candy, cookies, french fries, and such—you'll be on a fast track to improving your insulin and blood sugar levels, reducing your cravings, and bettering your memory.

Keeping insulin in check is critical to your overall mental and physical health. It's a hormone that helps determine how the calories you eat are used by your body. It is manufactured in the pancreas, which boosts production when you consume more simple carbs like sugar, processed grains, potato chips, and other foods that are quickly converted to sugar. When insulin levels are high, fat cells accumulate more and more glucose and fat. Staying on this kind of diet makes it impossible, practically speaking, to lose weight. The answer? Wean yourself off the insulin-boosting simple carbohydrates and replace them with hunger-satisfying, high-fiber, low-glycemic carbohydrates.

MEET THE GLYCEMIC INDEX (GI) AND GLYCEMIC LOAD (GL)

These two rating systems can help you make better food choices. The glycemic index (GI) ranks carbohydrates on their effect on blood sugar, using a scale of 1 to 100+ (glucose is 100). GI foods with a lower number tend to be healthier because they don't spike blood sugar; foods with a higher GI number are generally less healthy because they quickly raise blood sugar. In general, it's healthiest to stick with foods that have a GI value under 60. One surprising finding from the research: Table sugar is ranked lower on the GI than potatoes and bread!

Glycemic load is an even more valuable number because it takes both blood sugar and portion size into account. Pineapple, for instance, has a high GI (66) but a low GL (6). That means you have to eat a lot of pineapple to raise your blood sugar. A low GL is 10 or lower. Don't assume, however, that a food with a low GL is automatically good for you. Milk, for example, has a low GL, but it may be adulterated with antibiotics and hormones. To be sure your diet is healthy, check that the foods you are eating meet all the Memory Rescue Diet principles. (You can do an Internet search to find the glycemic index/glycemic load numbers for common foods.)

FIBER: A VITAL CARBOHYDRATE

Fiber is an unsung dietary hero. It provides a raft of health benefits, including balancing blood sugar, helping you feel full after a meal, reducing colon cancer risk, and keeping your bowels working smoothly. Yet most of us get far too little. The average American consumes less than 15 grams of fiber a day. The recommended amounts are 25 to 30 grams for women and 30 to 38 grams for men.

There are two types of fiber—soluble and insoluble. *Soluble fiber*, found in foods such as apples, blueberries, beans, oatmeal, and fiber supplements, helps prevent heart disease and diabetes. It also feeds the good bacteria in your gut, boosting immunity and helping limit the growth of bad bacteria. *Insoluble fiber*—what we think of as roughage—is found in seeds, stems, and skins. It helps keep the intestines cleaned out and distributes the critical by-products of soluble fiber throughout the colon.

Eating lots of vegetables will significantly increase your intake of both soluble and insoluble fiber. Fiber supplements can also be helpful, especially if you are insulin-resistant or have high cholesterol.

TROUBLESOME GRAINS

Many people look to breads and pasta as their primary sources of fiber. However, their health benefits are dubious at best. Sadly, the wild grains that our ancestors ate in tiny amounts bear little resemblance to the genetically hybridized grains produced today. I say *sadly* because our digestive systems are simply not equipped to process these modern grains—especially since the quantity we now consume has increased exponentially since the agricultural revolution began 300 years ago.

Modern grains are problematic in at least two ways. First, many of them turn to sugar in the body. And second, several—wheat, barley, rye, kamut, bulgur, corn, and spelt—contain glu- ten (the Latin word for *glue*), a sticky substance that gives bread dough its elasticity and helps it rise. Gluten has found its way into commercially made breads, cakes, cookies, cereals, pasta, and other grain-based products, as well as salad dressings, sauces, processed foods, and even cosmetics. And that has given rise to gluten-related health issues, including the autoimmune illnesses celiac disease, type 1 diabetes, and Hashimoto's disease. Gluten can also cause flu-like symptoms, psychological disturbances, acne, arthritis, and food addiction, and increase insulin resistance. And it can lower brain blood flow.[9] According to the Center for Celiac Research, 18 million Americans have gluten sensitivity, which can lead to more than 100 symptoms, including chronic diarrhea, bloating, flatulence, nausea, abdominal pain, skin rashes, fatigue, and mental fogginess.

Another troublesome grain is corn. Its unhealthy fatty-acid profile (high levels of omega-6 fats plus very low levels of omega-3s) makes it an inflammatory food that can damage the intestinal lining. Of particular concern is the widespread use of Roundup (a highly toxic glyphosate pesticide that is banned in some European countries) on US corn,[10] most of which is raised from genetically modified seeds.

Corn is ubiquitous in America, from corn oil to cornstarch to corn syrup and beyond, but you can greatly reduce your intake by avoiding processed foods and recipes containing corn kernels.

Say Good-Bye to Sugar

Arguably the worst carbohydrate in terms of your overall health is sugar. Per person, Americans eat about 140 pounds of sugar a year. Refined sugar is 99.4 to 99.7 percent pure calories, with no vitamins, minerals, or other redeeming ingredients. And don't be fooled: Whether it comes from a beehive, a maple tree, or any other natural source, it is still sugar. In the past several years, many sources have suggested that diabetics should use the sweetener agave because of its high fructose content (a staggering 80 to 90 percent). Fructose is often called a low-glycemic sweetener because, unlike sucrose, it doesn't cause insulin to spike. However, fructose is toxic to the liver and may trigger metabolic syndrome, fatty liver, and insulin resistance.

When you eat any form of sugar, your blood sugar spikes, your pancreas releases insulin, your blood sugar drops, and you long for something sweet . . . which restarts the cycle. Thus, when you eat sugar and simple carbs, you wind up craving them like a drug addict craves his drug.

Of course, that's just one of sugar's ill effects. Eating sugar and sugary foods increases inflammation and erratic brain cell firing, causes mineral deficiencies and weight gain, and has been associated with increased triglycerides, as well as lower HDL and higher LDL cholesterol. As for its impact on the brain, sugar consumption has been linked with depression, ADHD, hyperactivity, and increased slow brain waves in brain imaging studies. Research at UCLA showed that sugar affects learning and memory as well.[11]

ARTIFICIAL SWEETENERS: NOTHING SWEET ABOUT THEM

Consuming artificial sweeteners regularly is not a recipe for good health. It can contribute to chronically high insulin, which increases your risk for Alzheimer's disease and raises the risk of heart disease, diabetes, metabolic syndrome, and other health problems. It's a fallacy that artificial sweeteners help you lose weight; on the contrary, they may lead to weight gain because they may lower metabolism. The bottom line: Whether the sweetener is aspartame (NutraSweet, Equal), saccharin (Sweet'N Low), or sucralose (Splenda), it is better to avoid it.

ERYTHRITOL AND STEVIA: BETTER ALTERNATIVES

Erythritol, a sugar alcohol that comes in crystals or powder form, has no calories and doesn't lead to blood sugar or insulin spikes. Use it with caution until you know how you react to it since most sugar alcohols (such as xylitol and maltitol) cause GI distress.

Stevia, extracted from the leaf of an herb, is 200 to 300 times sweeter than sugar, but it does not affect blood sugar levels the way sugar does. In fact, it may stabilize blood sugar levels, enhance glucose tolerance, and lower blood pressure, but more research is needed. **Note:** Consult with a health-care provider before using stevia if you are taking medication for blood pressure or diabetes.

Hydrate with H_2O

If you are a man, roughly 60 percent of your body is water; if you are a woman, about 55 percent.

The percentage of your brain that is water is even higher: 80 percent. Water is essential for everything from lubricating your joints, flushing out waste products, and manufacturing hormones and neurotransmitters to regulating body temperature and helping deliver oxygen throughout your body. Not staying adequately hydrated has consequences for both brain and body: Research has shown that results in tasks requiring attention, memory, and physical performance are diminished when you are just 2 percent dehydrated.[12] The elderly, in particular, need to make a point of drinking water because the mechanism that triggers thirst can become less efficient with age.

Despite the often-repeated advice to drink eight glasses a day, the precise amount of water required to maintain adequate hydration has never been determined scientifically. From our experience at Amen Clinics, we advise drinking half your body weight in ounces every day. As an example, if you weigh 180 pounds, you should drink 90 ounces of water. However, if you are significantly overweight and calculate that your intake would be more than 120 ounces, consult a physician first; drinking that amount of water could trigger an electrolyte imbalance.

Staying adequately hydrated is especially important if you are losing weight. First, it helps prevent overeating. When you think you're hungry, you may actually be thirsty. Second, your body needs water to flush out the toxins released by stored body fat. Finally, if you drink two glasses (16 ounces) of water 30 minutes before a meal or snack, you can eat less and still feel satisfied. But dieting or not, avoid drinking water *with* your meals because it dilutes stomach acid, slowing digestion.

Just as important as downing enough water is limiting liquid calories and dehydrating drinks. Replace sodas (including diet sodas), fruit juices, and other sugary drinks with water. (You can either swap those calories for an equivalent amount of healthier food or cut them entirely and could lose 40 pounds in one year.) Avoid caffeine, alcohol, and other diuretics, and when you sweat during exercise, be sure to replace those fluids.

Flavor Your Food with Brain-Smart Herbs and Spices

It's easy to forget that herbs and spices are not just flavor enhancers but promoters of good health too. These plant-derived seasonings have a long history of medicinal uses that you can capitalize on in your cooking. Here are some of the most powerful memory-enhancing herbs and spices, along with a few of their benefits.

THE HERBS

- *Basil:* This potent antioxidant has been shown to improve blood flow to the brain, as well as improve cognitive function and prevent strokes.
- *Garlic:* Eating this bulbous herb increases blood flow and improves brain function. Regular consumption can help lower the risk of strokes and boost the immune system's ability to ward off colds and flu. Garlic can also help stabilize blood sugar and improve cholesterol levels.
- *Marjoram:* The lineup of nutrients in this

pretty, sweet-flavored herb is impressive—vitamin C, beta carotene, vitamin A, lutein, and zeaxanthin, which are known to protect against age-related degenerative diseases and cataracts. Marjoram also has anti-inflammatory and antibacterial properties.

- *Mint:* The scent of peppermint improves memory and focus, and its oils can soothe digestive upsets.
- *Oregano:* A superstrong antioxidant, oregano protects brain and body cells from free radicals that can cause premature aging. It may also ease insomnia and relieve migraine headaches.
- *Rosemary:* This well-known herb has both antioxidant and anti-inflammatory properties. It improves circulation and digestion and offers protection from the cognitive decline associated with dementia.
- *Saffron:* This herb appears to increase serotonin levels in the brain. Saffron can also improve memory and the ability to learn.

- *Sage:* Sage enhances memory and decreases the cognitive decline associated with Alzheimer's disease. The herb inhibits an enzyme that breaks down acetylcholine, a neurotransmitter that enhances memory at high levels.
- *Thyme:* This herb helps to protect neurons in the brain from premature aging. It also increases the amount of DHA in the brain.

THE SPICES

- *Black pepper:* This spice enhances the absorption of numerous compounds, including curcumin (a powerful antioxidant). It also increases hydrochloric acid (stomach acid), which aids in digestion.
- *Cayenne pepper:* The bold taste in cayenne is created by capsaicin, a well-known pain reliever. It, too, increases hydrochloric acid and helps lower inflammation, improve immunity, and stimulate metabolism. Be careful to moderate your intake if you suffer from hypertension.

- *Cinnamon:* This sweet/savory spice has been shown to lower cholesterol, fasting glucose, and HbA1c levels and improve insulin sensitivity. It has also been found to improve working memory in older adults and in prediabetic people while improving blood flow to the prefrontal cortex.
- *Cloves:* This fragrant super-antioxidant has had many medicinal roles over the millennia, from soothing upset stomachs and tooth pain to relieving diarrhea and acting as an expectorant. It also contains eugenol, a potent anti-inflammatory. The familiar dried flower buds of the clove tree are a popular flavoring in many Middle Eastern and Asian cuisines.
- *Coriander:* The phytonutrients in coriander may help control blood sugar and lower cholesterol levels. It is rich in manganese, vitamin C, and vitamin K.
- *Curcumin:* A polyphenol mix from turmeric root that is used in curry, curcumin is the primary curcuminoid in turmeric.

(Curcuminoids have been shown to decrease beta-amyloid plaques and inflammation.)

- *Ginger:* This spice has anti-inflammatory properties that may protect against neurodegenerative diseases and reduce the oxidative stress that causes brain cells to age and die. Ginger contains natural agents to help decrease nausea and vomiting, and it may help lower cholesterol. **Note:** Because of ginger's anticoagulant properties, check with your health-care provider before using ginger supplements if you are taking an anticoagulant medication.
- *Nutmeg:* This aromatic spice contains eugenol, a compound thought to protect the cardiovascular system. It also contains myristicin, which helps to prevent the formation of beta-amyloid plaques.

CHAPTER 3

EXERCISE YOUR BRAIN

USE IT OR LOSE IT. The old adage is as true of your brain as it is of your muscles. When you learn something, new neural connections are created, which improves your capacity to remember. In fact, regardless of your age, mental exercise has an overall positive effect on your brain. On the other hand, when you stop learning, cognitive performance suffers as the internal connections in your brain begin to break apart.

Neuroscientist Marian Diamond, PhD, from the University of California, Berkeley, spent four decades researching the brain, and her findings revolutionized our understanding of brain health and neuroplasticity. In a lecture to the American Society on Aging, she said, "We now know that with proper stimulation and an enriched environment, the human brain can continue to develop at any age."

Diamond and her colleagues reached that conclusion after studying middle-aged rats, comparable to 60-year-old humans, as well as older rats, some equivalent in age to people in their nineties. When the researchers provided the rodents with toys, balls, mazes, and other active rats to provide companionship, the size and cognitive ability of the rats' brains increased. This was evident from the sprouting dendrites, nerve cells, blood vessels, and the thicker cerebral cortex of their brains.

Dr. Diamond, who is now in her early nineties, summarizes the findings this way: "We can change the brain at any age. We're saying that if you use your brain you can change it as much as a younger brain." Although learning may take a bit more effort as we grow older, our brains can change for the better, especially if we keep them healthy with diet, exercise, challenge, newness, and love.

This chapter is about mental exercises that you can practice to keep your brain young and vigorous at any age.

Whole-Brain Workouts

The best mental exercises involve acquiring new knowledge and doing things you haven't done before. Even if your routine activities are fairly complicated, such as teaching a college course, reading brain scans, or fixing a crashed computer network, they won't help your brain as much as learning something new. Whenever the brain does something over and over, it learns how to do it using less and less energy. New learning, such as memorizing zip codes or learning a new game, helps establish new connections, thus maintaining and improving the function of less-often-used areas of the brain.

The parts of your brain that you use will grow, and the parts of your brain you do not use will atrophy, or shrink. That tells us something about how to exercise the brain. Just doing crossword puzzles or sudoku won't give you the full possible benefits. That's like going to the gym and leaving after doing right bicep curls. Here are some ideas for doing whole-brain combination workouts.

PREFRONTAL CORTEX (PFC) EXERCISES

- *Language games* such as Scrabble (if you memorize the Scrabble dictionary, you will crush your friends), Boggle, and Words With Friends
- *Crossword puzzles*
- *Speech and debate classes* in college; Toastmasters and other public speaking
- *Strategy games* such as chess and Risk
- *Tetris* (which also works the parietal and occipital lobes)
- *Prayer and meditation*, which may be the most powerful prefrontal cortex booster of all. I have published several studies on meditation, and I have seen how it reliably activates the prefrontal cortex.[1] It improves focus, executive function, judgment, and

impulse control, which results in more thoughtful and moral decisions.

- *Weight training and aerobic activity*

TEMPORAL LOBE EXERCISES

- *Three-dimensional video games*, such as Super Mario 3D World, lead to enhanced hippocampal function.[2] The added complexity and special dimension in 3-D games means players have more to explore and learn than in 2-D games, strengthening the players' learning and memory.
- *Intensive learning*, such as medical or law school, has been shown to increase hippocampal size after just 14 weeks.
- *Memorization of poetry and prose* increases hippocampal size.
- *Memory and mnemonic training* (see below)
- *Learning to play new musical instruments* strengthens the PFC, parietal lobes, and cerebellum.
- *Physical exercise* also increases the hippocampus. Learn a new sport as you are exercising for even greater benefit.

PARIETAL LOBE EXERCISES

- *Math games* like sudoku
- *Juggling*, which also involves the PFC, temporal lobes (hippocampus), occipital lobes, and cerebellum
- *Dance*, including the tango
- *Learning to read and play music*
- *Map reading* without a GPS device

BASAL GANGLIA EXERCISES

- *Balancing*
- *Synchronizing arm and leg movements*
- *Manipulating props* like ropes and balls

CEREBELLUM EXERCISES

- *Coordination games* like table tennis (which also involves the PFC), dancing, yoga, and tai chi
- *Basketball*

Learning has a very real effect on neurons: It makes it easier for them to fire and to continue firing. There are approximately a thousand trillion synapses in the brain, and each one of them may wither and die if it is not actively firing.

Like muscles that don't get used, idle nerve cells waste away. The brain has many different circuits connecting neurons in various parts of the brain. Any set of circuits that is not used grows weak.

Memory Strategies

Given all the information on conquering memory loss in this book, you may still be asking: *Are there specific exercises I can do to boost my memory?* Yes! BRIGHT MINDS is an example of a mnemonic, or a memory aid. It helps me immediately remember all 11 risk factors, so when I teach or talk about them on TV, I can sail through rather complicated material without any notes. It took my staff and me a while to come up with the mnemonic, but it was worth it.

I'd like to share three other memory magic tools that I've used with my patients and that I use myself to improve my ability to store and retain information.

1. **Rhymes are a very popular tool for recalling rules or organization.** As children, most of us were taught certain popular rhymes to help us learn to spell,

understand the time change each spring and fall, and familiarize ourselves with the number of days in each month of the year:

- "*I* before *e* except after *c*."
- "Spring ahead in spring; fall back in fall."
- "Thirty days hath September, April, June, and November; all the rest have 31, except February, which stands alone."

Rhymes help connect into a metrical pattern those items that otherwise may seem totally unrelated. They help establish a definite informational progression because any mistake in the order of recall will destroy the rhyme. Following is an example of using a nursery rhyme ("One is a bun; two is a shoe," etc.) to help retain a sequence of facts:

To use this mnemonic, choose 10 facts that you need to remember in a precise order, and mentally picture an association between each one and its corresponding number's object. In less than a few minutes, you can easily memorize their order. Try this method with unrelated facts to observe its usefulness to you.

As an example from my own life, here is a list of items I need to get at the store:

1. Salmon
2. Turkey
3. Unsweetened almond milk
4. Eggs
5. Stevia
6. Kale
7. Sparkling water
8. Spinach, olive oil
9. Oranges
10. Coconut

It took me about two minutes to make the following associations:

1. One is a bun: I picture a salmon trying to jump out of the bun.
2. Two is a shoe: A turkey walks around in colorful high heels.

3. Three is a tree: An almond milk tree drips milk on the kids below, who are crying.
4. Four is a door: Someone has thrown eggs at the door, and I'm really mad about it.
5. Five is a hive: Bees are flying around a stevia plant.
6. Six are sticks: A kid at the fair holds organic kale on a stick instead of cotton candy and refuses to eat it.
7. Seven is heaven: I am handed a flute of champagne, but since it is heaven, it is really sparkling water.
8. Eight is a gate: Popeye stands outside my front gate, eating spinach with one hand and picking up Olive Oyl with the other.
9. Nine is a line: Oranges are lined up for miles in Orange County, where I live.
10. Ten is a hen: A clucking chicken runs around the yard dressed in a bikini, with a coconut on its head.

Once I'm in the store, I run through these images in my head so I can remember the items I need to pick up—no written list needed. The more you do this exercise, the easier it becomes and the bigger your hippocampus may grow.

2. **Make words or phrases from the first letters of the words you need to remember.** When I have a series of facts to memorize, I immediately write down the first letter of each one to see if I can arrange them into an associative word or phrase. An example of this method:

   On old Olympus's towering top, a Finn and German viewed a hop.

   I learned this rhyme in medical school. Each first letter corresponds to the first letter of the 12 cranial nerves in their proper order: olfactory, optic, ocular, trochlear, trigeminal, abduceus, facial, acoustic, glossal pharyngeal, vagus, accessory, and hypoglossal.

   BRASS is used by marksmen to remember the steps in firing a rifle: breathe, relax, aim, stabilize, and squeeze.

3. **Use places to remember specific things.** This technique involves visualizing what you want to remember in a certain location. Then when you go back to the location in your mind, the object or fact should come back to you. For example, when memorizing a speech that you have organized and outlined, choose the ideas or the major subdivisions and associate them in some way with the different rooms in your home. As you deliver the speech, imagine yourself walking from room to room, discovering the associations you have made in the proper order.

   In order to make this effective, use these two tips:

    1. Make it active: Your brain does not think in still photographs, so the more action there is, the more details you can employ in a scene.
    2. Make the picture as crazy and disproportionate as possible: It will be easier to remember the details as you recall the strange or unique things in the picture.

If you practice this technique, your associative powers will become limited only by the number of locations you can think of. I imagine walking in my front door, then the living room, dining room, kitchen, family room, and so on. You can associate literally hundreds of items and ideas with the insides of most homes.

Use Your Memory to Feel Great Anytime, Anywhere

Many people struggle with anxiety and depression because they have trouble forgetting their fears, their frustrations, and the negative events in their lives. Their undisciplined minds constantly go to places of anger, regret, and sadness. Recognizing these tendencies in others, I have developed a memory technique that relies on the power of associations and places to help you feel great anytime, anywhere. Using your memory will help you counteract the negative and accentuate the positive.

Begin by writing down your best 10 to 30 memories of all time (constantly update them as new memories come into your life). Then peg them to specific places in your home or another location. Here is an example from my own life.

As of this writing, 12 of my favorite memories are

1. Marrying Tana and going on our honeymoon, which continues to this day
2. Being completely in love with our dog, Aslan, and cat, Miso
3. Helping my dad get well at the age of 87 and sharing his amazing story with the world
4. Having *Discover* magazine list our research on brain imaging as one of the top 100 stories in science for 2015
5. Eating dinner with my teenage daughter Breanne when she told me, "I kicked butt in a debate today, Dad"
6. Sitting at the dinner table playing strategy games with my son, Antony, when he was a child (he is now in his forties) and having him whip me
7. Having the world's most amazing, consistently loving mom

8. Standing at the stove with my grandpa when I was four years old
9. Being one of the chief architects with Pastor Rick Warren and Dr. Mark Hyman of *The Daniel Plan*, a program to make the world healthier through churches, done in thousands of congregations around the world
10. Watching my daughter Kaitlyn, now in her thirties, perform in *Pocahontas* in second grade
11. Sitting with my then-two-year-old daughter Chloe, now in her twenties, atop my shoulders at a Los Angeles Lakers game as she kissed my head and told me she loved me
12. Playing in the 1999 US Nationals Table Tennis Tournament

Walking through my home, here is how I peg these 12 memories to specific places using action and exaggeration.

1. At the front door—Carrying Tana across the threshold while she pleads for me not

to drop her. (I almost dropped her when we practiced our wedding dance the night before we were married. We still laugh about it.)

2. In the foyer—Aslan and Miso are always there to greet me when I come home, looking for love. Well, Aslan is always there, wagging his tail. You never know about a cat.
3. In the living room to the right of the foyer—My 88-year-old dad is in his workout clothes, doing jumping jacks, getting ready to go to the gym to lift weights. He once did a six-minute plank, completely dominating me. I wimped out at three minutes but was so proud of him.
4. In the living room, where we put our Christmas tree—My friend and research collaborator Dr. Cyrus Raji gave me a framed copy of our *Discover* magazine honor, where our research was listed as one of the top 100 stories in science for 2015.
5. In the dining room, next to the living

room—At the table I see my daughter Breanne as a teenager (she is now in her forties and the mother to two of my grandchildren). She winks at me and says, "I kicked butt in a debate today, Dad."

6. In the dining room at the dinner table—I see my son, Antony, playing strategy games with me when he was a boy. He is very intense thinking about his next move. He is so smart; he started beating me at them early.
7. In the kitchen, which smells amazing—My mom is making a tantalizing salad with lemon, olive oil, fresh crushed garlic, avocados from my dad's ranch, grilled lamb, and asparagus. She's excited to hear about my day.
8. In the kitchen, at the stove—My four-year-old self is standing on a step stool, smiling, next to my grandfather, after whom I was named. He was my best friend when I was growing up. He has on his white apron, and we are preparing sugar-free chocolate-and-cashew-butter

cups, a healthy, delicious version of the candy we used to make together. That way I can keep him with me longer.

9. In the kitchen, next to the sink—On the counter is a copy of *The Daniel Plan* and the accompanying cookbook. On top of the books, tens of thousands of tiny people are running around waving broccoli florets, symbolizing all the people who have undertaken our program.
10. In the family room, next to the kitchen—I see my then-seven-year-old daughter Kaitlyn in front of the TV performing in *Pocahontas*. She loved to perform, and being in front of the TV, blocking our view, never troubled her.
11. On the way upstairs—I see Chloe's room and imagine the zebra-hooded sweater she wore as she sat on my shoulders at the Lakers game, where she kissed my head and told me she loved me.
12. In my office upstairs—I see our Ping-Pong table, triggering the memory of the US Nationals, where I had a great time

> playing the game my mother taught me as a child.

Try this exercise on your own. Then anytime you feel sad or upset, walk through the house in your mind and trigger the positive memories, which in turn will release positive chemicals in your brain to help you feel great.

CHAPTER 4

FIND THE RIGHT MEDICATIONS

WHEN IT COMES TO addressing memory issues, there has been general disappointment with the medications currently available. None of them *cure* memory problems; they help only in the moment they are taken. Memory problems have too many causes for any silver bullet to do as much as was hoped. Yet pharmaceutical companies continue to spend billions of dollars with the hope of finding the next Prozac or Viagra. If we spent the same resources and scientific effort on prevention and lifestyle interventions, we would be much further ahead.

But medications do have a place and can be worth a try. If your memory problems are not responding to simpler interventions, talk with your health-care professionals about medications. In this section, I'll review several of the most common medications and explain how we use them at Amen Clinics.

Namenda (Memantine)

Namenda is approved for moderate to severe Alzheimer's disease. It has been shown to boost blood flow to the prefrontal cortex and, in some cases, delay the progression of the disease in its middle stages.

The drug modulates or partly blocks a receptor called N-methyl D-aspartate (NMDA), regulating the release of the neurotransmitter glutamate. This is important because excessive production of glutamate allows too much calcium to enter cells, which then turns on genes that are programmed to kill the neurons. (One take-home message: Don't overdo it with calcium supplements.)

Namenda sometimes produces substantial benefits in those with dementia. One of the more striking effects is the reduction in spasticity, which causes people to lose their balance, fall, or struggle to walk. Namenda can also help improve speech and fine motor skills, as well as reduce urinary incontinence. When Namenda is effective, the changes may be dramatic, easing the stress and burden on caregivers. Dosing usually starts at 5 mg a day for two weeks and is increased slowly to the maximum (typically 20 mg, although sometimes as much as 40 mg).

The Cholinesterase Inhibitors (Exelon, Razadyne, and Aricept)

As we age, acetylcholine, the neurotransmitter most often associated with memory, declines. Improving the availability of acetylcholine in the brain has been shown to help sustain memory. One way to do this is to inhibit the enzymes that break it down. These medications are called acetylcholinesterase (AChE) inhibitors, or "cholinesterase" inhibitors, and tend to work by increasing blood flow in the prefrontal cortex and temporal lobes. Three are prescribed most often.

Important differences among the cholinesterase inhibitors may determine how effectively they work in people with significant memory issues. Because acetylcholine neurons are found throughout the cerebral cortex, increasing acetylcholine can strengthen many abilities. These medications reduce behavioral problems and, in the earlier stages of Alzheimer's disease, improve attention, short-term memory, comprehension, communication, and the ability to recognize people and objects.

Early treatment is critical, since people whose abilities are already severely impaired do not see significant gains. I have treated many patients with significant memory problems who had symptoms for less than six months, and in these patients, short-term memory has often improved.

Many patients seek help for existing problems; however, just as important is delaying or halting the progression of the disease process itself. Exelon, Razadyne, and Aricept differ most in how they seek to slow the disease.

1. **Exelon (rivastigmine).** All three of these drugs block AChE, but only Exelon blocks butyrylcholinesterase (BuChE), the other enzyme that breaks down acetylcholine.[1] About 80

percent of the cholinesterase is AChE and 20 percent is BuChE in people who are aging normally. However, as Alzheimer's disease progresses, the amount of AChE decreases and the amount of BuChE increases to the point where they are about equal. Both AChE and BuChE must be blocked to stall the progression of Alzheimer's. At present, the only medication that does this is Exelon, which is why it is often my first choice, especially in the later stages of memory problems.

2. **Razadyne (galantamine).** Another option is Razadyne, which does not block BuChE and cannot raise the level of acetylcholine the way that Exelon can. However, Razadyne increases the levels of many different neurotransmitters, which generally increases brain activity.[2]

3. **Aricept (donepezil).** The first well-tolerated cholinesterase inhibitor produced in the United States, Aricept (donepezil) is now the most commonly prescribed of the cholinesterase inhibitors. Aricept is particularly effective in helping patients with mild Alzheimer's

disease, and patients report fewer side effects from it than from either Exelon or Razadyne. In addition, it needs to be given only once a day. Although its advantages make it attractive, particularly to busy physicians, it also has a couple of significant drawbacks that prevent it from being the first choice of many neurologists and psychiatrists.

Because Aricept (like Razadyne) does not block BuChE, it is less effective at blocking the accumulation of the beta-amyloid plaques. Aricept (like Exelon) does not bind to the nicotine receptor, so it does not increase overall brain activity as effectively as Razadyne, and it may not block programmed cell death.

Side Effects of the Cholinesterase Inhibitors

About 10 to 20 percent of people who take these medications experience side effects. For instance, some people become aggressive, but that often occurs with improvement in mental abilities. Fortunately, any aggression usually resolves within two weeks, and in many cases, families prefer not to stop or decrease the medication because their loved one is functioning so much better.

The primary side effects of Exelon and Razadyne are nausea, vomiting, loss of appetite, dizziness, lightheadedness or fainting, generalized weakness, and muscle pain. These side effects are not related to the stomach or heart; rather, they result from increasing acetylcholine activity in the brain stem. Groups of brain-stem neurons control vomiting (to keep you from swallowing things that will kill you), breathing, heart rate, blood pressure, and metabolism. Acetylcholine slows the heart rate, which causes a drop in blood pressure. The fainting, lightheadedness, or dizziness that results is usually not life-threatening and can be managed by reducing the dose of Exelon or Razadyne.

Aricept has similar side effects to Exelon and Razadyne, but they are less frequent. Aricept can also cause nightmares in some people who take it at bedtime. However, nightmares can usually be avoided by taking Aricept in the morning instead.

Stimulating Medications

Stimulant medications, such as Ritalin (methylphenidate) and Adderall (amphetamine salts), have been used to enhance focus, memory, motivation, and learning. They are classically used to treat children who have attention deficit disorder (ADD)—also known as attention deficit hyperactivity disorder (ADHD)—but I have had good success using them with people of all ages. They work by enhancing dopamine production in the basal ganglia and can increase blood flow to the prefrontal cortex and temporal lobes. If you have had ADD/ADHD symptoms throughout your life (short attention span, distractibility, disorganization, restlessness, and impulse-control issues), these meds are worth considering.

Because of the potential for addiction and side effects, Ritalin and Adderall are often not our first choices for patients with memory issues, but they should be considered if natural treatments are ineffective.

Provigil (modafinil) and Nuvigil (armodafinil) are commonly prescribed for narcolepsy. In many studies, they have also been found to heighten alertness and boost higher-order cognitive functions.[3] In my experience, these medications can help with energy, focus, and memory. They have fewer side effects than Ritalin and Adderall but also tend to have a milder effect. One of my ADD patients who could not tolerate Ritalin or Adderall was able to finish his doctorate on Provigil. He said it gave him sustained focus for six to eight hours.

Other medications, like selegiline (an antidepressant), reportedly have neurotrophic, or brain-enhancing, effects, but the research has been inconsistent.

I tell my patients that the issue should never be whether they are on or off medication but rather what supports their best functioning. If medications can help, I encourage patients to think of them like eyeglasses, which we would never withhold from someone who could benefit from them.

CONCLUSION

PLAN YOUR BRAIN'S FUTURE

CONGRATULATIONS! You have taken the first giant step on the journey toward strengthening and rehabilitating your memory, bettering your brain, and improving your overall health and well-being. If you opened this book worried because your recall wasn't as sharp as it once was, I hope you are encouraged, now that you have been introduced to dozens of ideas on how you can begin improving your memory *today*.

As I noted in the first few pages, having brain fog or trouble remembering things is not unusual, but you can do something about it.

You are not stuck with the brain you currently have. Many patients have come to the Amen Clinics with memory-related health issues and gotten serious about bettering their brains. Their determination and efforts to overcome significant challenges have inspired me, and their successes make me optimistic about *your* ability to address individual health problems and conquer memory loss.

Now that you've read about what you need to do, it's time to act on your new knowledge by putting together your personal plan to conquer memory loss. The next steps are up to you. Taking them may be challenging as you let go of familiar behaviors, but don't let that stop you. Focus instead on the rewards that await you: a stronger memory and improved health.

Here are my recommendations for your next steps.

Step 1: Assess Your Personal Risk Factors

First, you need to know the reasons for your current memory problems. That means you need to determine how your body and your brain are functioning right now. Here are some assessments that will provide you with this information:

- **A reliable cognitive test** (see page 147). A number of tests are available, but at Amen Clinics we use Brain Fit WebNeuro, which takes about 35 minutes to complete and provides an objective assessment of how your brain works in 17 specific areas. You can take it through our online Brain Fit Life program (www.mybrainfitlife.com). It produces a baseline score and, with retesting, a way to find out over time if your brain function is improving or deteriorating.
- **The BRIGHT MINDS risk factor assessment** (see page 153). This assessment provides you with two scores, one for your total number of BRIGHT MINDS risks and a second for your relative risks.

Step 2: Decide Which Risk Factor(s) to Address First

Once you have assessed the health of your brain and the rest of your body, you are ready to decide which risk factor(s) to focus on first. Chapter 1 explains these risk factors and how they are linked to memory issues. For each risk factor, I recommend a "checkup" of tests that will reveal problems related to that risk factor and a "prescription" of strategies designed to help you eliminate that particular risk factor. I presented a diet in chapter 2 that will help with the various risk factors. I recommend that *anyone* who has memory problems adopt a healthier diet based on the principles of this plan. And in chapters 3 and 4, I introduced strategies for memory workouts and potential medicinal interventions (as necessary).

Once you begin working to eliminate a risk factor, be sure to get follow-up testing after 12 or more weeks to track your progress. You also might want to jot down your healthy actions/activities in a daily journal or calendar and review them at the end of each day or week. Doing so will help you stay on top of your interventions, monitor their effectiveness, and see your progress more clearly. Research has shown that using a journal in this way will help you reach your goals.

If you prefer to concentrate on becoming healthier overall—or you simply want to take action while you await the date of a health exam or the arrival of test results—here is a quick-start checklist of actions that will reduce your risk in every BRIGHT MINDS category:

Blood flow

- ✓ Avoid anything that hurts your vascular health, such as caffeine or nicotine
- ✓ Drink more water
- ✓ Engage in regular exercise

Retirement and aging

- ✓ Spend 15 minutes a day learning something new
- ✓ Volunteer
- ✓ Try a daily 12- to 16-hour fast

Inflammation

- ✓ Floss your teeth daily, and care for your gums
- ✓ Eliminate trans fats
- ✓ Add omega-3s and probiotic foods or supplements to your diet

Genetics

- ✓ If dementia runs in your family, get early screening for memory issues
- ✓ Get tested for the APOE e4 gene
- ✓ Eat organic blueberries

Head trauma

- ✓ Do not text while walking or driving
- ✓ Be careful going up and down stairs—hold the handrail
- ✓ Always wear a seat belt when you drive or ride in a vehicle

Toxins

- ✓ Limit alcohol to two glasses a week
- ✓ Scan all your personal products with apps like Think Dirty
- ✓ Eat cruciferous vegetables for their detoxifying ability

Mental health

- ✓ Write down three things you are grateful for every day
- ✓ Take a walk in nature
- ✓ Pray to release your worries and to rejoice over the good things around you

Immunity/infection issues

- ✓ Start an elimination diet for a month to see if you have food allergies
- ✓ Watch comedies to boost your immunity
- ✓ Optimize your vitamin D level

Neurohormone deficiencies

- ✓ Eat more fiber
- ✓ Lift weights to boost testosterone
- ✓ Avoid hormone disruptors, such as BPA, phthalates, parabens, and pesticides

Diabesity

- ✓ Know your BMI (body mass index); if it's over 25, lose weight
- ✓ Start the Memory Rescue Diet in chapter 2
- ✓ Don't drink your calories

Sleep issues

- ✓ If you snore, get assessed for sleep apnea
- ✓ Turn off your electronic gadgets an hour before bed
- ✓ Listen to audio created to help with sleep

I would also add that, whatever your risk factors, you should take basic supplements daily for good brain and body health, including a 100 percent multivitamin/mineral complex daily with extra vitamins B_6 and B_{12}, folate, and vitamin D, plus omega-3 fatty acids EPA and DHA.

Step 3: How to Initiate Change—And Make It Stick

Making big changes can be daunting, and depending on your personal risk factors, you may discover you need to alter your lifestyle in a number of ways. If you find that you feel not only motivated by the challenge but also a bit apprehensive, it may help to acknowledge that this is a sizable undertaking that will take time, energy, and determination. That awareness can help you plot a strategy that works for you.

Everyone knows that the best intentions can easily go awry when obstacles arise. You set a goal to exercise three times a week, and it rains on two of the days you had earmarked to go outdoors for a walk. Temptation in the form of strawberry rhubarb pie—your favorite!—overwhelms your resolve to give up sweets. An ongoing work project interferes with your plans to get at least seven hours of sleep every night. Life happens, and you have to figure out a way to adapt and make headway toward your goals.

Here are some suggestions and science-backed tips that can help you maintain your resolve:

Plan first, and be specific. Reaching a goal is easier when you think about the what, when, where, and how of it before you put a plan into action.

Begin with small, measurable steps. They will build your confidence in your ability to reach your goals.

Write it down. Committing goals to paper (or the computer) reaffirms your determination to make changes. Post them where you will see them and be reminded (and motivated) to stick with your plan.

Make it routine. Repeating the same action or behavior over and over again in the same context until it becomes automatic (i.e., a habit) is one way to stay on track. A big side benefit is that once the action is automatic, you don't have to think about doing it and your brain is free to focus on something else.

Enlist family and/or friends. Share your intentions with one or more people who will support you, help you through any rough patches, and celebrate your successes. Be sure to call on them when your motivation flags or you backslide and find yourself tempted to quit.

Keep a journal (or use an app). Recording the actions you plan to take and checking them off when you have accomplished them will help you achieve your goals.

Mark it in your calendar. Incorporating change into your life usually requires making space for it. Enter commitments into your calendar and program alerts on your smartphone as reminders. Keep your family apprised of your commitments so that they can make any necessary accommodations and support you.

When tempted, say "I don't," not "I can't." Self-talk is an important part of staying the course. When you are confronted with a temptation, such as a glazed doughnut, research suggests that passing up the treat by saying "I don't eat doughnuts" is a better response than saying "I can't have doughnuts." The first is an empowering statement of self-control; the second implies a lack of choice and being constrained by forces outside yourself. Learning to say "I don't" is more likely to result in long-term success.[1]

Embrace your victories *and* your mess-ups. Keep looking back at what you have accomplished to build your motivation to move forward. That's more helpful than looking ahead at what still has to be done. And when you step off the path, forgive yourself and recommit to your goals as quickly as you can. Overcoming your risk factors and rescuing your memory rely on the accretion of small changes that you stick with over the long haul.

Lifestyle changes are at the heart of conquering memory loss. The reasons are twofold. First, prescription drugs have been ineffective at preventing Alzheimer's disease and other dementias. And second, well-designed scientific studies have shown that lifestyle interventions do work.

Don't wait. Begin today, right now, to conquer memory loss.

APPENDIX 1

MEMORY EVALUATION TOOLS

ALL OF US NEED a baseline brain health assessment to find out if our brains are in trouble. Unfortunately, this is rarely done. When I turned 50, my doctor wanted me to have a colonoscopy. I asked him why he didn't want to look at my brain. "Isn't the other end of my body just as important?" I asked. From colonoscopies and cardiac stress tests to mammograms and pap smears, baseline testing and preventive screening are done for most organs *except* the most important one—the organ that runs your life. That is just plain wrong, when illnesses like Alzheimer's disease are expected to skyrocket in the coming decades.

This appendix will explore the early warning signs of trouble, a simple computerized test that can help you evaluate your cognitive abilities, and the brain imaging tests we use at Amen Clinics.

Amen Clinics' Early Warning Signs Questionnaire

Rate each question on a scale of 0–4, from Never (0) to Very Frequently (4).

0	1	2	3	4
Never	Rarely	Occasionally	Frequently	Very Frequently

Memory issues

1. ___ Tend to be forgetful?
2. ___ Notice that your memory is getting worse?
3. ___ Misplace your keys or wallet?
4. ___ Wonder why you came into a room?

5. ___ Have trouble remembering names?
6. ___ Feel embarrassed by forgetting appointments?
7. ___ Read a book or an article but don't remember much of it?
8. ___ Have trouble remembering things that happened recently?
9. ___ Struggle with brain fog?
10. ___ Have trouble remembering to consistently take medications or supplements?
11. ___ Rely more and more on memory aids or reminders on your phone?
12. ___ Know something one day but forget it the next?
13. ___ Forget what you're going to say right in the middle of saying it?
14. ___ Have trouble following directions that have more than one or two steps?

15. ___ Suspect that your memory is worse than it was 10 years ago?

16. ___ Lose track of the conversation?

17. ___ Find things in unusual places, like your keys in the refrigerator?

18. ___ Get mad at others, thinking they took your things, only to find out later you misplaced them?

Trouble planning and problem-solving

19. ___ Have trouble making plans and sticking to them?

20. ___ Find it harder to follow a recipe or directions on how to put something together?

21. ___ Find it hard to focus on more complex tasks, especially those that involve math? For example, are you struggling with managing your bills or balancing your checkbook?

Confusion with times and places

22. ___ Have trouble driving to locations that had been familiar to you?

23. ___ Get easily confused or out of sorts?

24. ___ Get lost more easily or have to rely on GPS more than before?

Struggle with words

25. ___ Have more trouble finding the right word?

26. ___ Call things by the wrong name?

27. ___ Limit conversation with people rather than join in?

28. ___ Have trouble following along in conversations?

29. ___ Keep repeating yourself?

Worsening judgment

30. ___ Struggle with making more bad decisions?

31. ___ Make mistakes with your finances?

Social withdrawal

32. ___ Feel more isolated from friends?

33. ___ Feel like cutting back at work because you just don't care as much?

34. ___ Feel less interested in activities you usually find fun?

35. ___ Take less care of your physical appearance?

Scoring:

Add up the number of questions that you answered 3 (Frequently) or 4 (Very Frequently).

0	low risk of significant memory issues
1–2	mild risk of significant memory issues
3–5	moderate risk of significant memory issues
6+	high risk of significant memory issues

Of course, everyone should take brain health seriously. The higher you score, the more serious you should be. If you are at moderate to high risk, it is important to get a thorough medical evaluation.

A Reliable Cognitive Test

Several online cognitive tests can give you a sense of how well your brain is functioning compared to an age-matched group. At Amen Clinics, we use a comprehensive online test called Brain Fit WebNeuro that measures a wide range of cognitive and emotional functions. It takes about 35 minutes to complete and provides an objective assessment of how your brain works in 17 specific areas, scoring each one on a scale of 1 to 10. The test also generates an overall brain health score. Specifically, it measures

1. Motor coordination
2. Processing speed (how quickly you process information)
3. Sustained attention (ability to maintain focus)
4. Controlled attention (ability to stop reactions when needed)
5. Flexibility (shifting attention)
6. Inhibition (self-control)
7. Working memory (ability to hold information for short periods)

8. Recall memory (ability to remember information)
9. Executive function (ability to plan and organize information)
10. Identifying emotions (reading faces)
11. Emotion bias (impact of emotions on decision-making)
12. Stress level
13. Anxiety level
14. Depressed mood
15. Positivity-negativity bias (tendency to notice positive or negative emotions)
16. Resilience (coping during times of trial)
17. Social capacity (building and keeping relationships)

You can take this test through our online Brain Fit Life program (www.mybrainfitlife.com). It will provide you with a baseline score and, with retesting, a way to find out over time if your brain function is getting better or worse. Based on your scores, our program recommends targeted exercises in the form of fun brain games to strengthen vulnerable areas.

Determining the health of your brain with

baseline testing is a critical strategy for keeping it strong over the long run. If you are at moderate or high risk for memory problems, consider taking the Brain Fit WebNeuro test every few months to chart your progress. I also recommend everyone 40 or older take this test annually to spot issues early. Baseline testing and regular checkups can also help you uncover problems when they first appear.

Amen Clinics' Brain Imaging Tools

There are several ways to look at your brain if you are concerned about your memory. Most physicians will order an imaging study, such as an MRI or CT scan, which looks at the *structural* integrity of the brain. Most of these studies are read as normal, or as "mild atrophy (shrinkage) consistent with aging."

In my experience, *functional* brain imaging studies, like SPECT (single photon emission computed tomography), PET (positron-emission tomography), or QEEG (quantitative electroencephalogram), are more useful because *functional problems almost always precede structural ones*. These studies typically show problems before symptoms occur, which is when treatment is likely to be most helpful.

Functional studies are leading indicators of problems, meaning they show evidence of the disease process years before people show signs of it. Anatomical studies, such as CT and MRI, are lagging indicators. They show problems later in the course of the illness, when interventions tend to be less effective.

At Amen Clinics, we find two functional brain imaging studies particularly helpful.

1. Brain SPECT imaging: This scan looks at blood flow and activity patterns and shows us areas of the brain that are functionally healthy, underactive, or overactive.
2. QEEG testing: This scan shows the electrical activity in the brain.

Due to cost, PET scans are not commonly used, though they are sometimes used to detect plaques in the brain associated with Alzheimer's disease. For more information on SPECT imaging and QEEG testing, see www.amenclinics.com.

As I have written about in several of my previous books, one of the biggest lessons from our brain imaging work at Amen Clinics is that *all* psychiatric illnesses—including ADHD, anxiety, depression, and addictions—are not single or simple disorders in the brain; they *all* have multiple types that need their own unique treatments.

SPECT has taught us that memory problems are similar. Just as there are many roads to depression, so, too, are there many roads to losing your memory. SPECT can help in the diagnosis of different types of memory problems. Not only can it help diagnose Alzheimer's disease and other forms of dementia, it can also suggest mild cognitive impairment stemming from such causes as head trauma, infections, toxins, and depression.

APPENDIX 2

RISK FACTORS INVENTORY

IN CHAPTER 1, we looked at the risk factors for memory loss as well as steps to overcome each one. This inventory will help you to identify your particular risk factors. Mark the risks that apply to you. If you don't know whether you have a risk factor, refer to that factor's section in chapter 1 to learn more. When you get to the end of the assessment, add up your score. The number in parentheses next to each risk factor is the relative increase in risk for memory problems, accelerated aging, and Alzheimer's disease compared to those without that risk factor. Here's how it translates:

1.3 = 30 percent increased risk; 1.5 = 50 percent increased risk; 2 = double the risk, 3 = triple the risk, and so on.[1]

Blood Flow Risk Factors

1. History of a stroke (5)
2. History of cardiovascular disease, including coronary artery disease, heart attacks, heart failure, and heart arrhythmias (2)
3. Prehypertension or hypertension in midlife (2); low blood pressure in later life (1.3)
4. Erectile dysfunction (1.7 for all ages; 6.1 between 50 and 64; and 27.2 for men over age 65)
5. Limited exercise (less than twice a week) (2)

Retirement/Aging

6. Age: 65 to 84 (2), 85 and older (38)
7. Too much television viewing (more than two hours a day) (2)
8. A job that does not require new learning or retirement without new learning endeavors (2)

9. Loneliness or social isolation (2)

Inflammation

10. Periodontal (gum) disease (2)
11. Presence of inflammation in the body, indicated by high homocysteine or C-reactive protein (2)
12. Low omega-3 fatty acids (2)

Genetics and Family History

13. One family member with Alzheimer's or dementia (3.5); more than one family member with Alzheimer's or dementia (7.5)
14. One apolipoprotein E (*APOE*) e4 gene (2.5) or two *APOE* e4 genes (10) (if known, based on genetic testing)

Head Trauma

15. A single head injury with loss of consciousness (2)
16. Several head injuries without a loss of consciousness (2)
17. Loss of one's sense of smell (2)

Toxins

18. Smoking cigarettes for 10 years or longer (currently or in past) (2.3)
19. Alcohol dependence or drug dependence (currently or in past) (4.4)
20. History of radiation for head and neck cancers (3); chemotherapy for breast cancer (1.5), colorectal cancer (1.25), and possibly other cancers
21. Chronic exposure to heavy metals, such as lead, cadmium, mercury, arsenic, or aluminum (1.5)
22. Chronic mold exposure (1.5)
23. Kidney dysfunction (2)

Mental Health Issues

24. Post-traumatic stress disorder (4), bipolar disorder (2), schizophrenia (2), depression (3.5), or chronic stress (2)

Immunity/Infection Issues

25. Autoimmune issues, such as multiple sclerosis (1.5), rheumatoid arthritis (3), systemic lupus erythematosus (2), Crohn's disease (1.5), severe psoriasis (3)

26. Adult asthma (1.3)
27. Chronic Lyme disease or another infectious process in brain/body not fully treated (2)
28. Cold sores or genital herpes (2)

Neurohormone Deficiencies

29. Low in thyroid, estrogen (in females), or testosterone (males and females) (2 for each one)
30. Hysterectomy without estrogen replacement (2)
31. History of prostate cancer with testosterone-lowering treatment (2)

Diabesity

32. Prediabetes or diabetes (3)
33. Being overweight or obese in middle age (3)
34. Being underweight in older age (2)

Sleep Issues

35. Chronic insomnia (2.3)
36. Sleep apnea (2)

Total Score: Add up the total number of risk factors you have plus the total of all the numbers in parentheses (relative risk factors).

___ Total number of risk factors

___ Relative risk factors (the total score from the parentheses)

Interpretation of Relative Risk Factors:

If the score is 0–6: You likely have a low risk of developing Alzheimer's disease.

If the score is 7–14: You have a moderate risk; consider annual screening (lab tests, repeat of WebNeuro cognitive testing, and checkup with health-care provider) after age 50.

If the score is greater than 14: Consider annual screening (lab tests, repeat of WebNeuro cognitive testing, and checkup with health-care provider) after age 40.

NOTES

INTRODUCTION: THE TIME IS NOW

1. Cleusa P. Ferri et al., "Global Prevalence of Dementia: A Delphi Consensus Study," *Lancet* 366, no. 9503 (December 17, 2005): 2112–17, https://doi.org/10.1016/S0140-6736(05)67889-0.
2. "Who Has the Better Memory, Men or Women?" *ScienceDaily*, November 9, 2016, https://www.sciencedaily.com/releases/2016/11/161109112447.htm.
3. Miia Kivipelto and Krister Håkansson, "A Rare Success against Alzheimer's," *Scientific American*, April 2017, 32–34, https://doi.org/10.1038/scientificamerican0417-32.
4. Kivipelto and Håkansson, "A Rare Success," 32–34.
5. Brian Krans, "Dementia Drugs Ineffective at Slowing Mental Decline," *Healthline News*, September 17, 2013, http://www.healthline.com/health-news/mental-cognitive-enhancement-medications-dont-slow-mental-decline-091713#1.

6. Eric Rieman et al., "Brain Imaging and Fluid Biomarker Analysis in Young Adults at Genetic Risk for Autosomal Dominant Alzheimer's Disease in the Presenilin 1 E280A Kindred: A Case-Control Study," *Lancet Neurology* 11, no. 12 (December 2012): 1048–56, https://doi.org/10.1016/S1474-4422(12)70228-4; Yakeel T. Quiroz et al., "Brain Imaging and Blood Biomarker Abnormalities in Children with Autosomal-Dominant Alzheimer's Disease: A Cross-Sectional Study," *JAMA Neurology* 72, no. 8 (August 2015): 912–19, https://doi.org/10.1001/jamaneurol.2015.1099; Camilla Ferrari et al., "Imaging and Cognitive Reserve Studies Predict Dementia in Presymptomatic Alzheimer's Disease Subjects," *Neurodegenerative Diseases* 13 (August 2014): 157–59, https://doi.org/10.1159/000353690; Victor L. Villemagne et al., "Amyloid β Deposition, Neurodegeneration, and Cognitive Decline in Sporadic Alzheimer's Disease: A Prospective Cohort Study," *Lancet Neurology* 12, no. 4 (April 2013): 357–67, https://doi.org/10.1016/S1474-4422(13)70044-9.

CHAPTER 1: RECOGNIZE YOUR RISK FACTORS

1. For a more detailed look at each of these factors, as well as diet and nutraceutical suggestions, see chapters 5–15 of my book *Memory Rescue: Supercharge Your Brain, Reverse Memory Loss, and Remember What Matters Most* (Carol Stream, IL: Tyndale, 2017).
2. Y. Iturria-Medina et al., "Early Role of Vascular Dysregulation on Late-Onset Alzheimer's Disease Based on Multifactorial Data-Driven Analysis," *Nature Communications* 7 (June 21, 2016): 11934, https://doi.org/10.1038/ncomms11934; Marije R. Benedictus et al., "Lower Cerebral Blood Flow Is Associated with

Faster Cognitive Decline in Alzheimer's Disease," *European Radiology* 27, no. 3 (March 2017): 1169–75, https://doi.org/10.1007/s00330-016-4450-z.

3. Kamen A. Tsvetanov et al., "The Effect of Ageing on fMRI: Correction for the Confounding Effects of Vascular Reactivity Evaluated by Joint fMRI and MEG in 335 Adults," *Human Brain Mapping* 36, no. 6 (June 2015): 2248–69, https://doi.org/10.1002/hbm.22768.
4. "Dementia Risk Reduced by Putting Off Retirement, Study Suggests," CBS News, July 15, 2013, https://www.cbsnews.com/news/dementia-risk-reduced-by-putting-off-retirement-study-suggests/.
5. Karoline Lukaschek et al., "Cognitive Impairment Is Associated with a Low Omega-3 Index in the Elderly: Results from the KORA-Age Study," *Dementia and Geriatric Cognitive Disorders* 42, nos. 3–4 (2016): 236–45, https://doi.org/10.1159/000448805.
6. José A. Gil-Montoya et al., "Is Periodontitis a Risk Factor for Cognitive Impairment and Dementia? A Case-Control Study," *Journal of Periodontology* 86, no. 2 (February 2015): 244–53, https://doi.org/10.1902/jop.2014.140340; Jianfeng Luo et al., "Association between Tooth Loss and Cognitive Function among 3063 Chinese Older Adults: A Community-Based Study," *PLOS One* 10, no. 3 (March 24, 2015): e0120986, https://doi.org/10.1371/journal.pone.0120986.
7. Dennis J. Selkoe, "Alzheimer's Disease: Genotypes, Phenotypes, and Treatment," *Science* 275, no. 5300 (1997): 630–1, https://doi.org/10.1126/science.275.5300.630.
8. Kristen Dams-O'Connor et al., "Risk for Late-Life Re-Injury, Dementia and Death among Individuals

with Traumatic Brain Injury: A Population-Based Study," *Journal of Neurology, Neurosurgery, and Psychiatry* 84, no. 2 (February 2013): 177–82, https://doi.org/10.1136/jnnp-2012-303938.

9. Visit this link to watch a video of a newly autopsied brain, so you can see how soft it really is: "The Unfixed Brain," teaching video of Suzanne Stensaas, PhD, professor of neurobiology and anatomy, January 9, 2013, by the University of Utah Neuroscience Initiative, YouTube, 6 min., 18 sec., https://m.youtube.com/watch?v=jHxyP-nUhUY.
10. I. Konstantinidis, E. Tsakiropoulous, and J. Constantinidis, "Long Term Effects of Olfactory Training in Patients with Post-Infectious Olfactory Loss," *Rhinology* 54, no. 2 (June 2016): 170–75, https://doi.org/10.4193/Rhin15.264.
11. Lizzie Parry, "Head Rules Your Heart: Depression Is 'AS Dangerous as Being FAT—Causing Almost One in Five Heart Deaths,'" *The Sun*, January 16, 2017, https://www.thesun.co.uk/living/2627090/depression-is-as-dangerous-as-being-fat-causing-almost-one-in-five-heart-deaths/; Elizabeth Reisinger Walker, Robin E. McGee, and Benjamin G. Druss, "Mortality in Mental Disorders and Global Disease Burden Implications: A Systematic Review and Meta-Analysis," *JAMA Psychiatry* 72, no. 4 (April 2015): 334–41, https://doi.org/10.1001/jamapsychiatry.2014.2502.
12. Paul K. Crane et al., "Glucose Levels and Risk of Dementia," *New England Journal of Medicine* 369, no. 6 (August 8, 2013): 540–48, https://doi.org/10.1056/NEJMoa1215740.
13. Andy Menke et al., "Prevalence of and Trends in Diabetes among Adults in the United States,

1988–2012," *JAMA* 314, no. 10 (2015): 1021–29, https://doi.org/10.1001/jama.2015.10029.

14. Chun-Ju Chiang et al., "Midlife Risk Factors for Subtypes of Dementia: A Nested Case-Control Study in Taiwan," *American Journal of Geriatric Psychiatry* 15, no. 9 (September 2007): 762-71, https://doi.org/10.1097/JGP.0b013e318050c98f; Heidi White et al., "Weight Change in Alzheimer's Disease," *Journal of the American Geriatrics Society* 44, no. 3 (March 1996): 265–72, https://doi.org/10.1111/j.1532-5415.1996.tb00912.x.
15. Kristine Yaffe et al., "Sleep-Disordered Breathing, Hypoxia, and Risk of Mild Cognitive Impairment and Dementia in Older Women," *JAMA* 306, no. 6 (August 10, 2011): 613–19, https://doi.org/10.1001/jama.2011.1115; Yo-El S. Ju, Brendan P. Lucey, and David M. Holtzman, "Sleep and Alzheimer Disease Pathology—A Bidirectional Relationship," *Nature Reviews Neurology* 10 (2014): 115–19, https://doi.org/10.1038/nrneurol.2013.269; Wei-Pin Chang et al., "Sleep Apnea and the Risk of Dementia: A Population-Based 5-Year Follow-Up Study in Taiwan," *PLOS One* 8, no. 10 (October 24, 2013): e78655, https://doi.org/10.1371/journal.pone.0078655; Roxanne Sterniczuk et al., "Sleep Disturbance Is Associated with Incident Dementia and Mortality," *Current Alzheimer Research* 10, no. 7 (September 2013): 767–75, https://doi.org/10.2174/15672050113109990134; Ricardo S. Osorio et al., "Sleep-Disordered Breathing Advances Cognitive Decline in the Elderly," *Neurology* 84, no. 19 (May 12, 2015): 1964–71, https://doi.org/10.1212/WNL.0000000000001566.

CHAPTER 2: CONSUME THE RIGHT FUEL

1. Yian Gu et al., "Mediterranean Diet, Inflammatory and Metabolic Biomarkers, and Risk of Alzheimer's Disease," *Journal of Alzheimer's Disease* 22, no. 2 (2010): 483–92, https://doi.org/10.3233/JAD-2010-100897; Samantha Gardener et al., "Adherence to a Mediterranean Diet and Alzheimer's Disease Risk in an Australian Population," *Translational Psychiatry* 2 (October 2, 2012): e164, https://doi.org/10.1038/tp.2012.91.
2. Michelle Luciano et al., "Mediterranean-Type Diet and Brain Structural Change from 73 to 76 Years in a Scottish Cohort," *Neurology* 88, no. 5 (January 31, 2017): 449–55, https://doi.org/10.1212/WNL.0000000000003559.
3. Yipeng Wang and Eckhard Mandelkow, "Degradation of Tau Protein by Autophagy and Proteasomal Pathways," *Biochemical Society Transactions* 40, no. 4 (August 2012): 644–52, https://doi.org/10.1042/BST20120071; Qian Li, Yi Liu, and Miao Sun, "Autophagy and Alzheimer's Disease," *Cellular and Molecular Neurobiology* 37, no. 3 (April 2017): 377–88, https://doi.org/10.1007/s10571-016-0386-8.
4. Ben Spencer, "Why You Should NEVER Eat after 7 p.m.: Late Night Meals 'Increases the Risk of Heart Attack and Stroke,'" *Daily Mail*, August 31, 2016, http://www.dailymail.co.uk/health/article-3767231/Why-NEVER-eat-7pm-Late-night-meals-increases-risk-heart-attack-stroke.html.
5. Rosebud O. Roberts et al., "Relative Intake of Macronutrients Impacts Risk of Mild Cognitive

Impairment or Dementia," *Journal of Alzheimer's Disease* 32, no. 2 (2012): 329–39, https://doi.org/10.3233/JAD-2012-120862.

6. Yian Gu et al., "Nutrient Intake and Plasma β-Amyloid," *Neurology* 78, no. 23 (June 5, 2012): 1832–40, https://doi.org/10.1212/WNL.0b013e318258f7c2.
7. Kathleen A. Page et al., "Medium-Chain Fatty Acids Improve Cognitive Function in Intensively Treated Type 1 Diabetic Patients and Support In Vitro Synaptic Transmission during Acute Hypoglycemia," *Diabetes* 58, no. 5 (May 2009): 1237–44, https://doi.org/10.2337/db08-1557.
8. Beatrice A. Golomb and Alexis K. Bui, "A Fat to Forget: Trans Fat Consumption and Memory," *PLOS One* 10, no. 6 (June 17, 2015): e0128129, https://doi.org/10.1371/journal.pone.0128129.
9. Paolo Usai et al., "Frontal Cortical Perfusion Abnormalities Related to Gluten Intake and Associated Autoimmune Disease in Adult Coeliac Disease: 99mTc-ECD Brain SPECT Study," *Digestive and Liver Disease* 36, no. 8 (August 2004): 513–18, https://doi.org/10.1016/j.dld.2004.03.010.
10. Robin Mesnage et al., "Potential Toxic Effects of Glyphosate and Its Commercial Formulations below Regulatory Limits," *Food and Chemical Toxicology* 84 (October 2015): 133–53, https://doi.org/10.1016/j.fct.2015.08.012.
11. Elaine Schmidt, "This Is Your Brain on Sugar: UCLA Study Shows High-Fructose Diet Sabotages Learning, Memory," *UCLA Newsroom*, May 15, 2012, https://www.uclahealth.org/news/release/high-fructose-diet-sabotages-learning-memory.

12. Ana Adan, "Cognitive Performance and Dehydration," *Journal of the American College of Nutrition* 31. mp/ 2 (April 2012): 71–78, https://doi.org/10.1080/07315724.2012.10720011.

CHAPTER 3: EXERCISE YOUR BRAIN

1. Dharma Singh Khalsa et al., "Cerebral Blood Flow Changes During Chanting Meditation," *Nuclear Medicine Communications* 30, no. 12 (December 2009): 956–961, https://doi.org/10.1097/MNM.0b013e32832fa26c.
2. Gregory D. Clemenson and Craig E. L. Stark, "Virtual Environmental Enrichment through Video Games Improves Hippocampal-Associated Memory," *Journal of Neuroscience* 35, no. 49 (December 9, 2015): 16116–25, https://doi.org/10.1523/JNEUROSCI.2580-15.2015.

CHAPTER 4: FIND THE RIGHT MEDICATIONS

1. Taher Darreh-Shori et al., "Sustained Cholinesterase Inhibition in AD Patients Receiving Rivastigmine for 12 Months," *Neurology* 59, no. 4 (August 27, 2002): 563–72, https://doi.org/10.1212/WNL.59.4.563.
2. Máriton D. Santos et al., "The Nicotinic Allosteric Potentiating Ligand Galantamine Facilitates Synaptic Transmission in the Mammalian Central Nervous System," *Molecular Pharmacology* 61, no. 5 (May 2002): 1222–34, https://doi.org/10.1124/mol.61.5.1222.
3. Ruairidh M. Battleday and Anna K. Brem, "Modafinil for Cognitive Neuroenhancement in Healthy Non-Sleep-Deprived Subjects: A Systematic Review," *Eur Neuropsychopharmacol* 25, no. 11 (November 2015): 1865–81, https://doi.org/10.1016/j.euroneuro.2015.07.028.

CONCLUSION: PLAN YOUR BRAIN'S FUTURE

1. Vanessa M. Patrick and Henrik Hagtvedt, "'I Don't' versus 'I Can't': When Empowered Refusal Motivates Goal-Directed Behavior," *Journal of Consumer Research* 39, no. 2 (August 2012): 371–381, https://doi.org/10.1086/663212; Catherine Clifford, "3 Scientifically Proven Ways to Break Your Bad Habits," CNBC, January 6, 2017, http://www.cnbc.com/2017/01/06/3-scientifically-proven-ways-to-break-your-bad-habits.html.

APPENDIX 2: RISK FACTORS INVENTORY

1. For more on how each of these risk factors contributes to memory loss, see the notes to chapter 4 of *Memory Rescue: Supercharge Your Brain, Reverse Memory Loss, and Remember What Matters Most* (Carol Stream, IL: Tyndale, 2017).

ABOUT THE AUTHOR

Daniel G. Amen, MD, has helped millions of people change their brains and lives. He is the founder of Amen Clinics with 11 locations across the United States, a 19-time national bestselling author, and the creator of online videos about the brain and mental health that have been viewed nearly a billion times. He has written and produced 18 national public television specials about the brain that have aired more than 150,000 times across North America. Dr. Amen believes we can end mental illness by creating a revolution in brain health, and he regularly speaks to businesses, organizations, and churches about how to have a better brain and a better life.